Hack Your Bible

Sharpen Your Sword

v2.0

Hack Your Bible

Sharpen Your Sword

v2.0

P. Derrick Seagraves

Buy gift copies at www.HackYourBible.com

Contact the author at www.PDerrickS.com

Book Published as Series: April, 2013

First Compiled Edition: September, 2013

Second Printing: March, 2015

Second Edition: July, 2016

ISBN-13: 978-1536857009
ISBN-10: 1536857009

DEDICATIONS

Paul, Stephanie, Mercedes, and Porsche Seagraves - This family was made; it was crafted. Thank you for encouraging me through many false starts and failed attempts. Not everyone has as much backup as I do; I'm thankful to you. I hope to be as great a support to you as you have been to me.

Rev. & Sis. Mitch Glover - Your ministry inspired my final decision to make this the only path I'll walk. Your commitment to your calling, your preaching, your grace, and your love for people are epic.

Rev. & Sis. Frank LaCrosse - My family needed you. You have all of our respect and love, and your love for people defined a powerful church. I hear about you all across the country, though I'm not sure you ever left Washington.

Freebies for you.

- Printable End Resources
- Kid's Hacks
- Shareable Version of HYB
- Workshop Hand Outs/ Helps
- Video Demos

Go to http://eepurl.com/GHH_T

or scan this QR code for the form:

Sign up and we'll put the freebies in your email inbox immediately!

A quick note about the publisher:

KINGDOM PUBLISHER

is dedicated to the Apostolic Movement's growth. Our intention is to produce books of sound doctrine and lasting impact will out-pace the dredge.

Kingdom Publisher books are written by the best and most publisher supported authors. These authors break ground on new subjects and shed more light on the old. Our company is happy to pay them better, and support them further, than traditional publishing ever has.

We hope you will visit www.KingdomPublisher.com to find more excellent titles, or to publish your own work.

Thank you.

Please consider giving this as a gift

A portion of this book's sales will be donated to the Missionary efforts throughout the World Evangelism Center.

Also, support will be given to the wonderful (and free) Bible knowledge resource www.BLB.org

Thank you.

About the Author

P. Derrick Seagraves is an Alaskan UPCI evangelist and presently an elected official in the Alaska Yukon Youth Ministry. He enjoys investing in young people, Biblical preaching and teaching, and the outdoors.

As Alumni Secretary of Indiana Bible College he promotes the school and connects with Alumni. As a self-published author he also created the publishing process found at www.KingdomPublisher.com.

If you would like to read Derrick's writings, be updated on his ministry and projects, or connect personally, please visit www.PDerrickS.com

CONTENTS

NOTICES

NOTE ON COPYRIGHT

Hell is hot. Use your best God-given judgment. Don't help people steal this Christian guide, there is a free version available at : www.HackYourBible.com

NOTICE ON PRAYER

When in doubt, pray. It's like washing your hands. Reading scripture? Pray. Sharing your faith? Pray. Have heartburn? Yup, you guessed it; pray. Too much prayer is like being too clean- there might technically be a danger there, but most of us will never see it. Pray more.

NOTICE OF LIABILITY

No party affiliated with or distributing Hack Your Bible in any form takes responsibility or liability for your actions or the actions of third parties. This is an educational resource, meant to inform. Please don't ruin an heirloom Bible, damage other property, or yourself; that would make us both very unhappy.

NOTICE ON INTERNET RESOURCES

Our full curriculum is within the covers of this book. For those of you who want to "go beyond" in your research, I have provided good footnotes and links to Internet resources. But Internet resources change frequently, despite our best efforts.

So, for various reasons the links may not direct you to the resource intended. In many cases you will likely be able to use your favorite search engine to locate the correct link. If links to a good resource are not easily found, or are missing completely, and avid readers notify us we will do our best to support you with those resources again in posts or pages at www.HackYourBible.com.

:Intro:

I believe this book is needed.

"Bible Hacking" is about getting the most out of God's word, and making it more usable. Your Hacked Bible will be full of unique changes that make it your own. You'll have the resources to defend your faith anywhere, the context to study better, and the kind of access to knowledge that usually takes years to recall at your fingertips.

Essentially we want you to become a super-Christian.

My greatest hope is not for you, though.

It might seem odd to hear, that in writing to you my hope is for another, but this is true. I want you to know your Bible better, and for you to make it infinitely more useable in your daily life, for the purpose of saving a lost and dying world. There are people all around you, everywhere, that need to hear the message of hope and salvation contained in those pages.

Maybe if you are more familiar with your Bible you'll be more confident in sharing it. Maybe if you read it more, you might live like you believe it. Hopefully if you are asked to teach, or lead in anything, your hacked Bible will become an invaluable resource. I pray that you use it daily. I especially hope that while hacking your Bible you will allow it to influence you more in life and decisions.

A good gunsmith can take a firearm that you are good with, and craft it into a weapon that is so perfectly in tune with your body and shooting style that you will never sell it. I'm not your gunsmith, but I want to help you make that weapon. If you're not comfortable with your Bible then it's less likely you'll become proficient in using it. Let's build something epic.

There's a lot of tricks in this series for marking truths in the Bible and making them super easy to find. There's a lot of methods to get extra out of your reading, and to make reading super easy. If you are teaching and preaching there are even more little tricks to make your life easier. I'm not the originator of all of these hacks, but my passion for getting more from the Word of God has pushed me to find and collect these to share with you.

You might use this series to break in a new Bible. You likely won't use all the hacks but I hope that in making the book cheap enough I'll have given you an introduction to what is available for your Bible.

//Five Reasons to Read HYB//

1. You probably don’t know your Bible well enough.

I didn’t. I realized that thought I had strong beliefs I couldn’t find them in the Bible quickly. They were there, but I had no access. As a Christian under the Great Commission, that needed to change. I need a Bible that not only contains truth but has it highlighted and underlined, indexed and linked. That is what I built here in Hack Your Bible. There was no book like this before.

2. Bibles produced today are weak.

These bare-bones, no options Bibles are fitting for today’s popular “just enough” Christianity, but we want more! Where is the depth, and the tools to go beyond just follow where someone else is speaking from? You need to know how to craft features into your Bible that you will actually use. You also need to know how to care for and fix your Bible as it wears. This book is a guide in that direction.

3. You don't believe what everyone else does.

The "Bible helps" produced today cater to someone other than you. In-Bible commentaries and notes appeal to the largest segments of traditional Christianity exclusively. We even have some "translations" (they're not really translations, but paraphrases or commentaries) that will support whatever special interest you like. There's a gay "Queen James Bible," and a "Green Bible" that attempts to undermine and re-define what the Biblical dominion of man is.

But you; you know what you believe. Your Bible should reflect that. Your Bible should be ready to shout its truth. Your Bible should be a testament to the fact that you have researched and proved your faith through the scriptures.

4. You don't have time to build a Bible system.

I don't want you to waste time; I want you to pull ahead of the pack. This guide is how I'll help you. I'm offering systems for building your own resources, really. Yes, I offer a *lot* of resources here in the HYB series, but what I *really* hope is that you see the systems behind it. Then as you learn you can continue to make your Bible better, well beyond the scope of this guide.

5. There is a commission on you, a calling on your life.

The Old Testament Law said "love God," and Jesus called this the greatest commandment.

Then He said the second greatest commandment was like it; "love people."

I believe that Jesus, God walking on Earth, went on to later combine these when He commanded "Go ye into all the world, and preach the gospel."[1] If you really love God, you'll bring the people He loves back to Him. If you really love people, you'll reconcile them to their God and salvation.

You can build a great Bible to help change the world with. You need to know God's word, and to have ready access to the parts that will make a difference to people in the moment.

---

[1] Mark 16:15

//How to use HYB+//

I'm very excited to present this guide series. I hope it will start a revolution of new Bible-thumpers! Congratulations on getting in on the revolution and please: *Read all instructions for a hack before you attempt any hack.*

Please also share this series, and show off your Hacked Bible, to everyone you can

Don't worry about outgrowing the notes you write in your Bible someday. Know that you can (and probably should) buy another Bible whenever it is you need to move on, and you'll hack that one too. You'll then have a happy memory-maker on your shelf, a history of your spiritual development.

These hacks are presented as complete lessons with supplies named, references lined out, and processes detailed. It's my experience that some people like to know the shortest route to being finished, while others what to stay awhile and know the "why."

So for each hack I will write out: why this is important, how you will use it in the future, maybe share a story, and then outline exact step-by-step and efficient methods to completing the hack.

You are, of course, free to change whatever you like as you use these hacks. I hope you improve on these first ideas, and use all of them.

If you feel you've made an improvement on a hack and want to share it with the community, just contact me through HackYourBible.com *There is also a Facebook page and lastly, we can chat via Twitter, my handle is @PDerrickS*

:Mods:

[Enter story:]

The summer of 2011 I was given two Bibles from giants of the gospel. The first was from my dying grandfather, Paul C. Seagraves, affectionately called "Papa."

I was home in Washington visiting him as his health faded. In his final years he let on that he was reading the Bible five times a year, and in visiting with him I learned his prayers were constant. A lifetime of service was culminating to the moment that he would meet his savior.

He had started many churches, pastored many more, helping heal and grow congregations through America's South and up her West Coast. The last church he started, constructing a building out from his own business, was in Seattle, WA. That was the only one I ever knew as a child.

In starting that church he had bought a pair of

Thompson Chain Reference Bibles, high quality black leather ones, for his assistant pastor and himself. This was a new chapter, an adventure, and they logged their notes as they studied for these people and presented the truth.

Papa Marked that Bible up. He wrapped it in a cover, he added tassels, he made notes, and left mementos for his future self to be reminded of powerful and changing times. He didn't mean to create inspiration for his grandson, but while he weakened he gave that Bible he pastored Seattle out of to me.

Papa's zipper hack:

I was always aware that Papa was an extremely practical man (he preferred to live in a 5th wheel trailer, so that nothing would hold him back from going and preaching). One thing that stuck out to me was how he had hacked his Bible cover. It's a convenience and I didn't know where else to put it; but you might use it so I'll include it here.

If you have a Bible cover, and ever "lose" the zipper in the folds of the cover, you'll like this. Papa had run a keyring through his zipper on the cover. In this way there was always a ring you could put a finger through to pull the zipper closed. And the zipper is never turned around and out of reach. All my covers are outfitted with this hack now; thanks Papa!

The second Bible I was given was from the man that pastored my family for more than 20 years. Retired, and resting from a career in ministry, he continues to attend church with my parents. Like a grandfather to me himself, he had sold off his businesses and horses and gone into the ministry in his 40's, and started pastoring our church in Tacoma, WA at 50. Later he married my parents together, and dedicated me as a baby. He baptized me, and led my family through the challenges that life brings. He built the largest youth-group in our district, and one of the greatest church families I have ever even heard of.

He sat me down and told me that he was proud of me deciding to preach, and that he wanted me to have his Bible. He also said that if I ever decided to betray the gospel that I was raised in he wanted it back. That Bible was also wrapped in a cover, filled with notes and finger stained pages, pictures of him and his wife, highlighting, sermon texts with notable preachers and the dates they were preached from, and full sermons written in the back.

I was already forming this book at the time I received these presents, but they showed me that great Christians make their Bibles their own. I was onto something!

Don't be afraid to modify your Bible; you're in a great tradition.

If you look at older Bibles, like in your pastor's office (or even the thrift store often times) you'll see many improvements above and beyond the Bibles at your local Christian bookstore. In an age where everything has seen enhancements and major improvements, our Bibles' construction has been neglected. It's a shame that you don't have to live with.

So let's make them awesome. No need to go buy a $300 custom bound Bible- you can make what you already have meet your needs better than anyone else. Modding the Bible is fun and exciting.

//Marker Ribbons//

You might have seen high end, thick, study Bibles with multiple markers (often in multiple colors.) This is an extremely useful feature for your personal study and later when you decide to share the truths you've found. You can have a marker for your personal reading, one for where your Bible study left off, and several for your sermon texts while preaching. Having built in "markers" means they can't fall out, and the different colors allows the ribbon markers to be designated for a subject or to correlate with your notes (each scripture referenced in your notes could be highlighted with it's ribbon color.)

The benefits of a muti-marker Bible are so great that I think every Bible should have at least 3. There's no reason that only huge, expensive Bibles 9that you wouldn't actually carry) should be the only ones benefiting from these features. Often this feature means that the Bible you're looking at has a price tag over $150 and includes a lot of other options like a concordance, maps, a study and reference system, and others making it quite thick. You might not want this thickness, or all of these additional resources. Here is your solution.

You can install your own ribbon markers, in whatever colors you like, for less than $5 at a fabric store.

Marker ribbons: Method 1

Our first method is the easiest, but not always available. Some Christian book stores sell a strip of cardboard or plastic that has ribbons attached at the top. You can purchase this and then slide it down the spine of your Bible and it's done! This method might slip out, but you can glue it in place with one drop.

Make sure that the ribbons will reach at least 1 ½ inches below the page once installed. If they don't then your ribbon might not reach far enough when you try to use it to flip to the spot you saved. The marker might also slip up into the pages, inaccessible, if it's not long enough.

Another downside to the pre-made option is that often the ribbon is not wide enough. You want a ⅓" to ½" ribbon, and many of the store-bought ones are not that wide. This means that the ribbon may twist and roll or fold between the pages creating odd creases and possibly damaging the spine, if the ribbons don't lay flat. These possible downsides bring us to the DIY method, which I prefer.

Marker ribbons: Method 2

Materials:

- Scissors
- Clear fingernail polish
- Three to five colors of ⅓" ribbon that are twice as long as your Bible is tall
- Super glue
- A small scrap of thin cardboard (like a cereal box)
- Small, sharp knife/ razor
- Cutting surface

Step 1

Cut the thin cardboard into a strip ¼" thinner than the binding of your Bible and 4" long. Make sure you're cutting on a surface that you don't mind damaging, and if you need help ask for it. We want to be ale to praise God with all our fingers intact!

Step 2

Test that the strip you've just cut will fit between the cover and the back of the pages. If it is snug cut another ¼" off the edge, as you need to fit your ribbons in this space eventually as well.

Step 3

Using the knife (like an exacto knife) on the cutting surface (like a cutting board) slice a ⅓" slit in the middle of the cardboard, 1" from what will be the top. Then do the same 2" from the top. [see image]

Step 4

Repeat Step 3 for however many ribbons your are using, spreading out from the center and staggering ½" [see images on the next page for examples of both a 3 ribbon cut pattern, and a 5 ribbon cut pattern.]

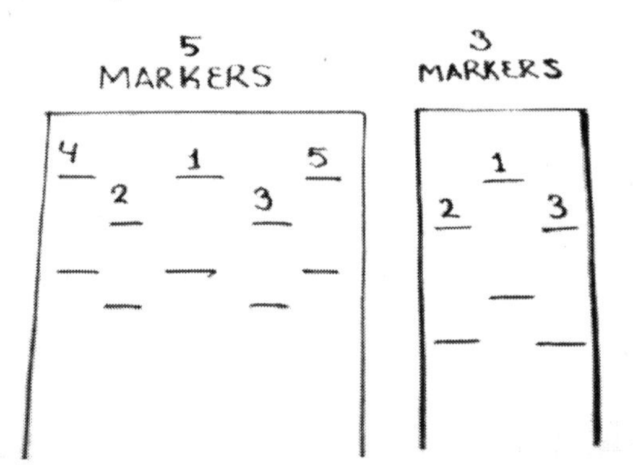

Step 5

Fit each ribbon into a series of slits, folding it over

and gluing it at the end. [see image] You might be able to use two ribbons in one slit.

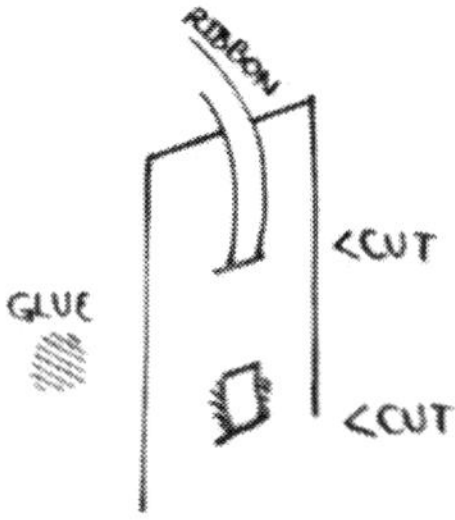

Step 6

After giving the glue time enough to dry (maybe a half hour) slip the insert into the binding, between the cover and the paper.

Step 7

Now pull the ribbons through the pages, like you're marking a spot, and cut them 2" from the bottom of the page. Leaving this extra allows you to use the ribbons much easier.

Step 8

Take the ribbons and cardboard out of the book completely and use the nail polish to paint the ends of the ribbons so that they will not fray. You will only need to paint the last ¼", if that, with a very light coat. You might use the glue if polish is not accessible. Let these dry for 15 min.

Step 9

Apply 4 good globs of glue to the base of the cardboard insert, opposite from the side the ribbons come out from. Now insert the cardboard with the glue facing the bound pages and the ribbons exiting the cardboard toward the cover.

Ribbon Marker Conclusion

If you have done these steps correctly, you now have glue a little smeared up along your cardboard and binding drying, and when you pull down on a ribbon it tends to pull the plastic or cardboard down into the book's binding, rather than pulling it out of the book as it would if reversed. [see image]

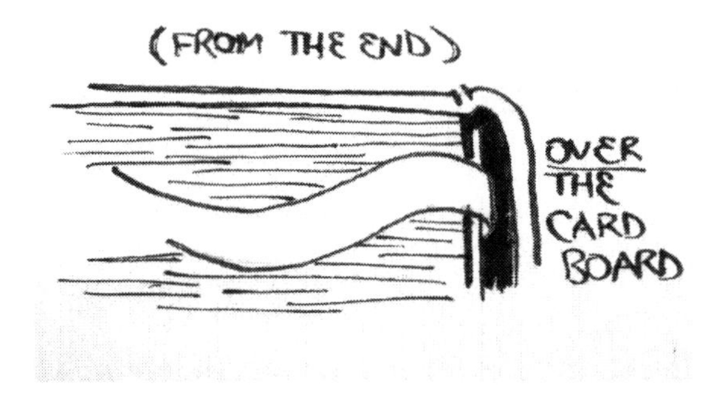

Congratulations!

You now have hacked your Bible in a useful and fun way. You will enjoy the benefits of having more markers, but you will also enjoy having a one-of-a-kind Bible. I hope you take pride, and please consider helping someone else do this to their Bible too.

Online, Live Demo Video!

Through the power of the internet, we are able to hack videos into books! Using your smart-phone please scan this QR Code (there are many free QR apps) to see our YouTube video showing every step of this hack as demonstrated by the author. We hacked a Bible to give to a nursing home resident who was getting a Bible study.

If you can not scan this QR Code, then just type this URL into your browser;

http://kaywa.me/cpu9a

...or search www.YouTube.com for

"Hack Your Bible demo: the Ribbon Hack"

//Inserting Material//

If you wish your Bible had a resource that it doesn't, you shouldn't necessarily start shopping. No Bible, in my experience, has all the attributes you would like in the way you would like them. And if you did find that perfect Bible your needs would change eventually. However, you will likely be able to find or format any resource you want and put it in your current Bible after this hack. Some ideas for resources you might include in your hacked Bible come later in this section.

Inserting Material: Method 1:

The easiest way I know to add a resource would be to copy the notes from another resource onto the blank pages in the back of your Bible (why did you think they were there?). You should line them with a pencil and ruler so your notes are not sloppy. You could even the lines later. Those pages will fill up fast, though, so I'm offering another option.

Inserting Material: Method 2:

You might take a very thin (ie: a Moleskin cashier) notebook and write your resources into it. This will take time, but you will again know the material better because you have written it yourself. I feel it's worth it. Then glue the back of the cashier notebook into to back of your back cover.

The biggest downside to this second method is that the cover of the cashier notebook is stiff, almost always. In a soft covered Bible, like a nice calfskin, this will not work. It will make a nice leather cover hard like cardboard.

Materials:

- Mechanical pencil
- Cashier notebook
- Hairspray
- Glue *

* Super Glue works, but there are much better options for serious Bible lovers. Find these later in this book under *"HYB //Sys and Repairs"*

Step 1

Locate resources. These can be found in Bible encyclopedias, commentaries, your sermon notes, the back of your friends' or parents' Bibles, or of course HYB+

Step 2

Write these out in your cashier notebook. I would use a mechanical pencil for it's small lines and the ability to erase.

Pro note: Artists "seal" pencil sketches with a light coating of hairspray to keep them from smudging. You could do the same on your notes here

Step 3

Glue the outside of the notebook's back cover to the inside of the back cover of your Bible.

Note

I would not use more than one cashier notebook, as you can harm a Bible's spine by over stuffing it's covers. Cracking can happen in the glue, or tears in the stitching, and then you start losing pages. Think about this whenever you use your Bible as a filing cabinet for notes, church handouts, 10yr old wedding invites, and pens/ pencils.

Inserting Material: Method 3:

The page-by-page method. This is great because you can simply print or copy whatever resource you like to the right size! If you do write out the reference then installing it this way will allow you cover to remain soft and pliable, depending on the paper and glue you use.

Depending on the format of the page and margin area left on the page you can either fold and glue the edge, or add a folded strip of paper to attach the page. By folding the edge of the page you can have an area to glue (or even tape), but also a nice and durable fold. If there is not enough margin, and folding will keep you from being able to read it all, then fold a strip of paper and glue it to both the inside of the Bible and the page.

Materials

- Glue
- Super Glue works, but there are much better options for serious Bible lovers. Find these in the later book of our series *"HYB //Sys and Repairs"*
- Paper to attach with
- Scissors
- Mechanical pencil
- Ruler
- Resource (printed and cut to the right size)

Step 1

Cut the strip of paper 1" wide and as tall as the long side of your resource

Step 2

On a surface you can spill glue onto, glue the paper strip to the back of your printed-and-cut resource with the Super Glue.

Step 3

While Super Glue is drying, use the ruler and pencil to draw lines for additional notes on the back of the resource, These should be ⅝" apart from each other.

*** Do not close the Bible while the glue is drying and glue your Bible shut! ***

Step 4

Once the strip is attached to the resource, fold the strip in half "hot dog" ways (not "hamburger") and apply glue to the back of this strip, effectively the same side that is attached to the resource. Then stick this onto the cover or page that you've decided to attach the resource to. [see image on next page]

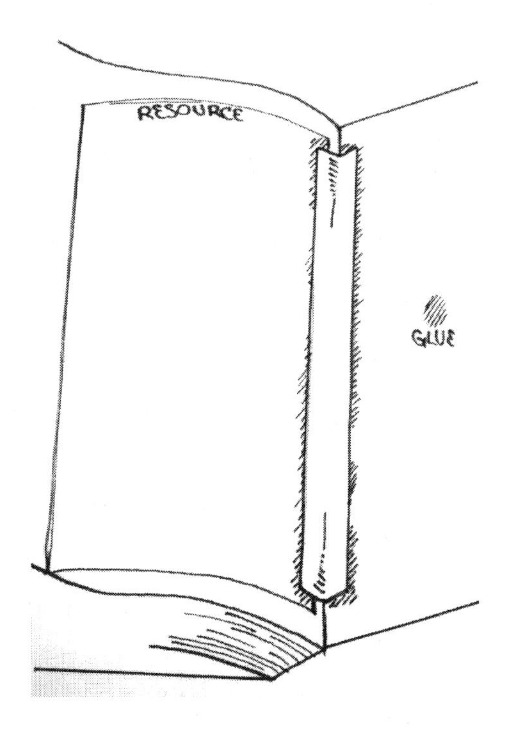

(Note: That spot of glue is not to be applied there, but you give you reference of how I drew the glue: with shaded lines)

In this way you will be able to add the resources in HYB+ along with whatever else you find valuable. Of course you can add a cashier notebook and also add pages from this method, like printed maps or guides, at the same time but again be warned of the damage over-stuffing can cause.

Lastly,

you could hybrid these ideas. You could glue a cashier notebook in, and then tape or glue resources into the inside of that. Or you could add resources to your sermon journal. This last version is my preferred method, because my sermon journal is my Bible's constant companion and I don't mind the high maintenance of copying resources into each journal I use. But I'm a preacher and I'm dedicated to this.

Whatever you decide to do learn to collect good resources. They create context for our study and give a depth that reading alone wouldn't bring. How far did Israel travel by foot, from Egypt to Canaan? How far did Paul take the gospel? What is a "dragon" in the Bible? How valuable is a "shekel" of silver? Your resources don't all have to be found in your Bible or Journal, many resource books are useful and can be kept on a shelf#. You want to keep the most valuable and useful ones at hand, though.

... What to insert

We talked about how to insert a page, it's pretty simple, but now we should look at what would be valuable to insert.

The reason to insert a page or resource into your Bible is really dependent on your ministry, and what it is you're working on as a Christian. These are likely going to be added to, or removed, even more in the future.

The very first thing to insert is an "Index of Hacks." You can probably just dedicate a blank page in the front of your Bible to this and write them it. This is where you will record what Hacks you have finished or are working on, and where to find them. You can write what verse your built-in Bible Studies start with, or what different highlighter colors mean. Really you just don't want to forget what it is you have done to this Bible.

Next there is a group of inserts called "context builders." Context is the reason some Bibles have maps and cultural notes. The Bible isn't Science Fiction, set on another planet; it is a history of what took place here on Earth. The Bible records stories from the Middle East, South and Western Europe,

Near Asia, and North Africa. These places had other names then, and your maps should connect our current names of places with the Biblical ones. Now you'll see how far it is Mary traveled pregnant with Jesus, and where all Paul took the gospel. With that in mind, make sure your maps have the missionary journeys of Paul, and Jesus, and the major churches marked. If they don't then draw those in, in different colors, with a note there what color is what.

At the end of this book is a free reference to some of the greatest Bible maps ever made.

Time-lines are also great for building context. I didn't know this until looking at a time line, but the pilgrims were landing in America just before the King James Version of the Bible was being printed! That kind of comparison is what a time-line is good for. Compare secular histories with the Biblical accounts you will and gain a lot, especially with the new testament and early church. Then you'll have a setting for the scripture.

Bible studies should also, always, be included! We have some studies that you can build into your Bible through highlighting and reference marking (called "chain referencing" see the chapter here), but others are going to need an introduction and many scriptures with notes for explanation.

These more involved Bible studies, on specific

subjects like Angelology[2] and the History of the Jews, are just too much to write into your margins. You might, for the sake of space saving, put these into your Bible Journal.

"Key Sheets" can be made on other denominations and religions. How you can connect with them, differences, their common arguments, holes in their beliefs, verses that conflict with their beliefs, questions to ask, and answers to give are all great areas that should be covered. Atheist/ Agnostic, Baptist, Muslim, and Catholic keys are a must in America. You can make these by reading some books on the subject, making an outline with the key points covered from each book, and then condensing these into a reference sheet. You don't have to be an expert, just knowledgeable enough to be backed up by experts and their books.

For you, though, those are already made and available on page 90 of this book!

The Essential Doctrines of the Bible published by Pentecostal Publishing House is excellent. I taught my first 4 months as youth pastor almost exclusively out of this resource. Such things as "the Doctrine of God" and "Holiness and Christian living" are covered,

---

2 You guessed it, the Biblical study of Angels: what they are, and what the can and cannot do

in much detail and with a lot of scripture. If you want to know why Christians believe what we do it's a good investment.

You can buy the book and carry that, or likely better, you can abbreviate the most important subjects to you into a size that will fit in your Bible. They will be a great help in sharing what you believe either way. You can find my abbreviation of these doctrines ready to in the back of the book. Just make sure you read through the scriptures and points made as soon as you get them so that you can know how to present them.

Something every preacher might keep: outlines of Evergreen Sermons[3] and illustrations. I am in no way a fan of pre-canned preaching, and strive to be fresh in preparation and prayer at every speaking opportunity. However, we are not always given much time to prepare a lesson or sermon. I have been asked to "preach something valuable" with less than a 1/2hr to prepare. For these cases you might have some material in your Bible ready. Many would likely leave these on a laptop, but we don't travel with laptops to church as often as we do Bibles.

I'm not offering any resources on sermons for you

---

[3] Evergreen in the sense that they are ready in any season, like an evergreen tree.

to preach, sorry; pray and study for those.

//How to insert tabs, and when not to//

Tabs mark the books of the Bible like sticky-notes hanging off the edges of the pages. If you are not super familiar with your Bible tabs are the best way to keep up with a preacher's fast scripture changing. In small groups you'll be able to keep pace with the lesson. When teaching a Bible study you will be able to help your study partner find scriptures because you'll be there already, in a flash. Some look down on tabs, but that is superficial and that should not dissuade you. Use all the tools to be the best you can be all the time.

There are pre-formatted tabs that are a good option, your can buy them in most Christian bookstores or online[4]. They act like stickers and you just find the first page of that book in the Bible and stick the tab there. There will likely be instructions, but your tabs should descend like this. [see image]

The home style DIY options are better if you want to be able to remove the tabs later, once you are more familiar with you Bible's layout. The pre-formatted ones are prettier but meant to be

---

[4] Found cheap on Amazon http://www.amazon.com/Bible-Tab-Clear-Center-Lettering/dp/9900493303

permanent.

You can make tabs yourself with stickers, or post-it-notes if you like. Even tape, folded over itself and written on, is a good option. There is a list in the front of your Bible that will give you the correct order, often page number, and spelling of the books. There are common abbreviations also; you may need to look online for those to make marking the tabs easier.

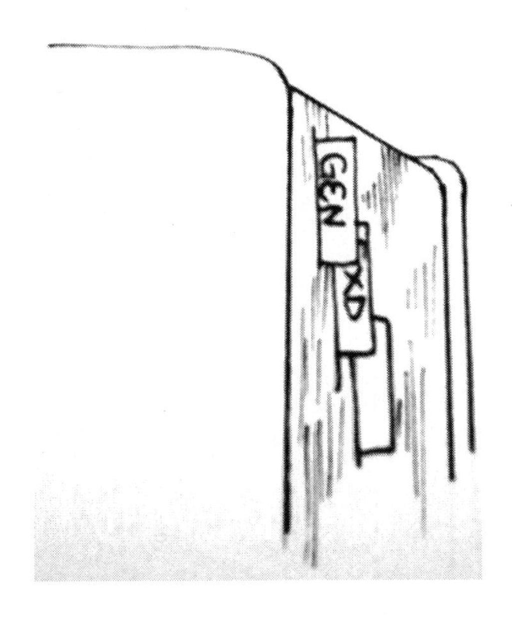

//Theme Your Bible//

Themes are found throughout scripture, and it is valuable to know what and where they are. Understanding themes in scripture allows us to very clearly define principles, like the character of God or the nature of sin. In the future you will be able to share these themes with others to encourage them and very quickly share the truth of the Bible.

The best way I have found to keep these at hand is "theming" your Bible. Consider making this a group project that brings a group closer to their Bibles and each other.

Essentially to Theme a Bible you take all the scriptures on a subject, and color code them with highlighting both in the verse and on the edge of the page, so they're easy to find. All the edge markings are in the same spot on the pages so that when one bends the edges of the pages back all the page markings are shown. If a scripture is used for more than one topic, you can highlight in one color, underline in another, border in yet another, or even highlight half and half.

Some ideas for subjects and themes:

Oneness of God*	Commandments
Necessity of Baptism*	Prophecies of Jesus*
Holiness*	Judgment
Heaven	Promises of God
Hell	Prophecy + Fulfillment in the Bible
What is the Holy Ghost*	

All of those that have a * next to them are included in the back of this book as a reference sheet, we're proud to say! You can take these pages of verses and theme your Bible quickly, without having to do all the research for the scripture on the topic.

These lists are a culmination of several other lists found online, and formatted in the way I found best. I hope they're a blessing!

Theme Your Bible Hack:

Materials:

- 4 Highlighters
- 2 Scrap pages of paper (not torn)

Step 1

In the front cover of your Bible, on the first blank page, write the subject you are highlighting right now and highlight it in the color you will be using for that subject. Use only this highlighter for these scriptures

Step 2

Find the scripture referenced in your list to be highlighted, read it, and make sure you understand immediately how that scripture talks about the subject you are highlighting for.

A lot of the lists you will find are "fluffed" with extra scriptures. These scriptures might have a deep Greek meaning to the list maker, or extra-Biblical reference. They might be forced to have an out of context meaning. In the end: Don't highlight the scripture if you don't get why it matters to your theme!

Step 4

If you can explain why this verse matters, then highlight that. Maybe tweet it or post it out there too, if you're not ashamed.

Step 5

Take one piece of your scrap paper and put it under the right page's right edge, sticking out so you cannot highlight the next pages. It does not matter if the highlighted verse is on the left hand page, we always mark the right hand page so there is only one way to fold the pages of your Bible. You do not want this highlighting to accidentally mark the next page. It fouls the whole system.

Step 6

Line up the next scrap page with the top of the page of the Bible, and ¼" from the right hand edge.

Step 7

Highlight from the scrap paper onto to Bible page continuing to the other scrap paper so that you have highlighted all the way to the edge.

Now you have a type of template on the top scrap paper. If you always line up with the top edge of the

Bible page, you will always highlight the same spot. Now you can really theme your Bible, and other subjects won't bleed into each other. I suspect you could research all the subjects suggested and theme them all on one Bible.

Step 8

Repeat Steps 2-7, reading each scripture and judging, then highlighting in the right color, and consistently marking the edge of the page, until you have exhausted your list.

*Bonus

In the future, if you find a scripture that supports one of the themes you have marked, you can always highlight that one the same way. There's no end to this system.

If you have a series of scriptures you would like to share with the Bible hacking community please contact me at www.PDerrickS.com I would be happy to pass your research along, or maybe you could write a guest post?

#MakeThis a GroupProject!

Every youth-group can use these Bible Hacks to improve their understanding and ability with the Bible. It's a great team building exercise that can take just one meeting, or could be a series for your small group meetings. We're confident that you will see your group more excited about their Bibles.

We are adding some free emailed resources for you to have a successful hack-a-thon. Make sure you sign up for them at http://eepurl.com/HYBFreebies

Now your group can be confident in their Bible knowledge. Their faith is secure because they have marked in their Bible where they can support their doctrine.

Great job!

//Bible Journal//

Journal writing has been the mark of great leaders.

Ancient kings had servants whose entire job was to journal their days, called scribes. Lawyers, powerful businessmen, and politicians hire specially trained secretaries to journal their thoughts. For mariners it is a serious responsibility. Here is a short list of great people who kept journals with many, many, great people omitted:

- Theodore Roosevelt
- Thomas Jefferson
- Ann Frank
- Benjamin Franklin
- Lewis and Clark
- Andrew Carnegie
- Ralph Waldo Emerson
- Captain Cook
- Winston Churchill
- Sir Edmund Hillary

- Sir Ernest Henry Shackleton

There are many reasons to journal as a Christian.[5] Maybe you want to **be immortal**; this is the easiest way. After you die your children and grandchildren will look into your life, and know you as a person, through your writings. The process of writing in a journal creates present mindedness.

This might sound Zen, but contentment and defining where you are instead of constant striving is Biblical. You will write things that you will want to remember; markers in your life are recorded in a journal and made more vivid in the future this way.

All of these are good reasons to have a personal journal, but we are talking about a Bible journal. Here you would write spiritual things and notes too large, abstract, or specific for the margins of your Bible. You'll record for the future what the Bible is saying to you today.

While reading the Bible in your personal devotions, whether simply reading or working on a reading program, you will **receive insight**. This is

---

[5] A great book on Christian journaling is "Spiritual Disciplines for the Christian Life" by Donald S. Whintney

God's living work you are taking in, and when it speaks you should record it. You will see verses in new lights. You will see support for themes and truths you didn't know of before. And as you mature you will want to see how.

If you see a theme developing, or a connection between scriptures, those are worth recording. Don't think "someone else has already seen this." Even if your observation is not completely original, this is your journal and story, and what you're seeing is worth recording. I have been consistently amazed at the people that come to me after I speak and say "I never looked at it that way." I'm just recording what I get in study.

Sermon notes are what take up most of my Bible journal. I outline nearly every sermon I hear. I scribble inspiration for my own sermons. I note when a scripture is used in a new way than I have seen before. I write out how scriptures are linked together to make a point. I write down facts and illustrations.

Whatever catches my interest in a sermon goes into my sermon notes, in my Bible journal, for me to keep and use in the future.

Testimonies are another must. Write out every testimony you have; I write the testimonies I am told of first hand also. These faith builders are a great help in later times when your prayers and Bible reading seems a little cold.

Write troubles too. Hardships and questions you have are testimonies in the making. If you read something that doesn't make sense, write that down! Then speak to your pastor, but write it down immediately so you don't forget. Why let a question linger? Conflicts can kill your spiritual self, don't let them pop up and then dismiss them; they're like ivy cracking up a brick home. Trap them in your journal and kill them whenever you can.

If you are enduring a personal struggle it helps to write it down and define it. Also, later, you'll find verses that deal with your situation, and you'll be able to reference them to that entry from before. When God comes through you have a live history of God working in your life! I cannot describe how wonderful it is to read back and see **the testimonies of what God's done** for me. The truth is, though, I might do like Israel did and forget God's goodness if I had not have wrote the trial down.

You should record your **Bible studies and outreach progress** somewhere. A Bible journal is perfect for this. You can record dates and subject covered, record the questions they had (especially if you don't think you gave a perfect answer and want to ask someone else later,) and major points in their conversion like baptism and first church attendance.

This way you'll see that you are making progress, and you'll be encouraged.

Prayers should also be kept in here. This might sometimes fall under the "troubles" section just before this, but not always, so I wanted to pull it out for you to focus on. **If you're praying for something write it down**. If you get something, an insight or word from God or burden, definitely write that down! If you're praying for your future spouse, or for a better job, or for a soul in need; keep that in faith that it's a testimony in the making.

How to format your journal:

Step 1

Make sure every page is numbered; this way in the future you can easily index the journal's best parts for reference. You could use dates, but those are going to be all over, and some days you'll write 5 pages and others just a line. You don't have to buy a numbered journal, but make sure there are numbers there before you start writing.

Step 2

Date every note you write, and not just with the "Month/ Day/ Year" but with the day of the week as well. This gives context to your future self when reviewing your journal.

Step 3

Have a symbol for each type of entry. These may be a star, a cross, praying hands, a dove, an * or @ or ^ even. This way, in the future your review will be faster. Definitely at least title the entries as "Sermon Idea" or something. If you do use symbols write what they mean as a legend in the front of the journal.

Step 4

Review your journal periodically and make an index of major entries in the front of it. If you have numbered your journal then you can have subjects like "Testimonies" and then the page numbers to find them. You may even use a highlighter and color coordinate the index to the entries.

Step 5

Have at least one ribbon marker. Add more if it will help you.

Step 6

Don't' be afraid to draw.

Step 7

When recording a sermon use outline format, like this:

I. Scripture

A. Point made from it

B. Second point made from it

1. Application

C. Supporting scripture

Step 8

Use underlining, scribbled circles, bolding, and boxes to make a big deal about big things. How will you know what is important in the future?

Also, for your enjoyment, here is a sample journal page:

2-17-13 R. K. Rodenbush @ Calvary Tabernacle

Eph: 2:13 You were afar off

1 Pet 1:18-19 but His blood saved you

-Davinci Code - says the "secret" is that Jesus wasn't who He said He was

-The problem is that it undermines and disqualifies salvation

-"I shredded it! And I decided: I'm going to preach about the blood more than ever!"

-(Has "Nothing but the Blood" sang)

^ He does something fun here, he preaches over the song

-The Blood changes us, it's a hope that doesn't fade, it's an anchor that holds...

** Sermon Idea: Psalm 1 is a contrast of the world's systems of finding success in life, and God's way. 1 Jn 2:15-17 makes it more plain - there is only one way to define, and achieve, lasting success: God's way*

Thoughts inspired: I was praying for a sermon today, and God reminded me of all the times He's come through. It was powerful to have blessing after blessing flow out and into my mind. It's unbelievable the distance in mindset, and in region that God's brought me. I can know for certain that He is going to take me the rest of the way.

Money's tight right now- but there was a time I was laid off for months and somehow I kept getting odd jobs and opportunities all around the youth work I had dived into. I wound up making more on those odd jobs that I usually did with a salary, and I got to minister too! ...(the end)

Last thoughts on Journals

One of the main reasons you should keep a journal, for your Bible or self, is that it cements facts and stories in your mind. If you have gone to school in the last ten years it is likely that you have experienced "multi-sensory education." To help students retain what they are supposed to be learning teachers are including more senses. Instead of only hearing a lecture, now we do worksheets and watch a sideshow. In younger grades they even use smelly markers and snacks to reinforce lessons.

You can take advantage of this same tool in journal writing. You are forced to reprocess something to be able to record it. If you record in paraphrase, or in diagrams, even better. This reprocessing makes you "get it" before you can record it in your own way. If you think for a moment you'll understand this.

You can find a *great* reading plan called the "5 x 5 x 5" in *"HYB // Apps"* the next book in this compilation. It integrates your journal and reading plan into one great system. In this way you'll be building two great habits at once.

//Sticky notes//

You might find this silly, but I keep sticky notes in both my Bible and Bible Journal. It's easy to do: you take off a short stack and then stick the back of these notes to the inside of the cover. Just make sure the stack isn't more than 1/8th in. thick, for your binding's health.

With these notes you can make extra notes in your Bible than your margins can handle. You can put last minute reminders on your paper sermon notes. You could also add to your journal entries. Any time you need a scrap of paper it's handy; that's why sticky notes are in every office.

You can use these to place explanations next to your scriptures. Your can line up key points in a row on a series of notes. Also, you can set up a sermon by marking the verses in your Bible, although ribbons are more elegant.

To do this:

Step 1

Tear/cut a sticky note into a few strips .

Step 2

Locate the verse and place the strip of sticky note

so that the verse is sticking out and easy to see.

Step 3

Label them with what number order you'll use them in. Then write those same numbers in your notes and your have an easy to follow trail of scriptures.

//The Built in "Chain Bible Study"//

Have you ever known someone that knew their Bible SO well that they could give a Bible study at the drop of a hat? They make you marvel at their knowledge, and maybe they inspire you to know your Bible better. I know my pastor inspires me!

It's hard to achieve that level of knowledge, though. But here and now we are going to use a shortcut, a hack, to be able to give a Bible study at any time you have your Bible.

Here's the hack: You take a list of verses that compile a Bible study (you can find 4 free ones included in the End Resources!), and connect them in a chain by referencing from one to the next in order. You can add whatever notes you need to explain the verse by writing next to the referencing. Since every Bible study is a progression of scripture this chain is easy to make out of almost any shorter Bible Study.

How it goes:

Step 1

Write in your Hack Index the name or subject of the Bible study, the initials of the Bible study in parentheses, and the first verse in the chain.

Step 2

Go to the first verse in the chain, write the initial of the study, and the reference to the next verse with an arrow > pointing the direction to the next verse in the chain.

Step 3

If you need a hint, or want to make a note for future help, this is the time to write it in the margin near the verse.

Step 4

Locate the next verse. Write the initials for the study, the previous scripture in the chain with a / in front of it (this means “close” in HTML) and then a reference to the next verse in the chain with a arrow in the direction < .

*Example: (One God)

OG

/Gen 1:1

Deu 6:4>

Step 5

If you need a note, write it down.

Step 6

Repeat Steps 4 & 5 until the chain is done

The Chain-Bible-Study is my favorite hack.

You now have the ability to teach a Bible study wherever you have your Bible. If you keep it in you backpack, or bag, you'll be able to give a solid Bible study, quickly and without fail. You can build in many, great Bible studies on many, important subjects.

This hack would make a great group project

If you want to get a group together, like a youth-group, and do this hack together then we have a great option for you. We can offer bulk purchasing discounts, just contact the author at www.HackYourBible.com

Or you could just invite me to do a workshop!

:Apps:

What good is the Bible if it is never applied? It is a waste of God's revelation for it not to be used in our lives and spread to others'. This book in the HYB series is all about you applying the Word.

For too long we have treated the Bible as a reference book. We act like it's a dictionary or encyclopedia, and only crack it's covers to find that one quote or the topic we're interested in. But it's more than that - the Bible is the history of God's interaction with humanity. And that interaction continues today. Will you let it in your life?

By applying the Word we reach into God's unchanging nature and principles. During prayer in the past I have been reminded to search the Bible for my answer. And there it is, my answer, written a thousands of years ago sometimes. The Bible is powerful if applied, and exalted even above God's name![6] Why would you not use it?

I hope you understand and use these hacks to their fullest purpose: evangelism! Yes; these are going to make you a stronger Christian. You will of course be mighty in the word and supported by the power found in it as you apply God's revelation to your life. But the church has a purpose, and it's not spiritual body-building; we are called to reconcile the world to it's loving creator.

With His words in your heart, and backed up with a Hacked Bible, you can meet the needs of this dying generation. Is there any family untouched by addiction or self loathing, hate or impurity? Will you search your Bible for the answers to these needs, and apply it to them? You can be that "true Christian" that pulls families from the depths of this world's despair.

Learn the doctrines unchanging and without conflict. Build yourself B0ible studies that are a part of your Bible and travel with you. Actually read your Bible every day - I'll help you right here in this book.

You can be that real Christian. You can have a Bible that proves your faith and is unflinching in it's stand. You can back yourself up and take pride,

---

[6] Psalm 138:2 "I will worship toward thy holy temple, and praise thy name for thy lovingkindness and for thy truth: for thou hast magnified thy word above all thy name."

teaching others and leading them from the power of God's revelation. Follow on.

//Essential Bible Doctrines//

Is there truth? The real Christian says "yes," and that it can be found in the Bible. There are non-negotiable doctrines that all must abide by to live in correct relationship with God. This is a fundamentalist statement - but that is what our movement is based on. We stand on the authority of the Bible rejecting anything else that raises itself to challenge it's supremacy.

This is an outline format of points made about doctrine, and the scriptures supporting them. It is a quick reference to what the Apostolic Movement believes and where to find them in the Bible. Headings include: An Inspired Bible, Doctrine of God, Identity of Jesus, Angels and Demons, Biblical Salvation, and Christian Living.

You may choose to copy these points into the blank note pages in your Bible, or print the pages and fold them to keep in your Bible by following the Inserting Material chapter in the sister book "Hack Your Bible/ Mods."

This resource could be worth all the cost of HYB+ to you alone. Use it. Share these; even among your own church group. Many of these scriptures are taken from the excellent "Essential Doctrines of the

Bible" by David K. Bernard.[7]

Essential Bible Doctrines

God Is

- The very first verse of the Bible introduces God as the Creator. Gen 1:1
- Society and conscience proclaim God Rom 2:15,
    1. Ultimately Faith is needed Heb 11:6

The Bible is God's word, through inspiration and preservation

- It has unique and correct ancient claims on science, history, and geography
    - The Bible says the world is round, before science did, in Is 40:22 (just one example of about 35 science proofs) [8]
- The Bible's self claims

---

[7] Found at http://www.amazon.com/Essential-Doctrines-Bible-David-Bernard/dp/0932581285/ref=tmm_pap_title_0 (not and affiliate link, I make no $ if you buy this)

[8] Further reading online: http://www.clarifyingchristianity.com/science.shtml

  - The Bible is "God breathed" according to 2 Tim 3:16
  - The Bible was written "as the Spirit moved them" 2 Pet 1:21
- The integrity of Jesus and His endorsement of the Old Testament

  Mat 5:18-19
- And many more secular proofs of the Bible:
  - The testimony of many peoples, and their secular contemporaries in History
  - It's moral superiority to alternative "holy texts"
- It's unity, despite 40 writers and 1600+ years in it's making
- The lack of any credible alternative
- It's accurate preservation, despite many attempts of destruction
- The influence on society
- The life changing power in it's texts
- The fulfilled promises and miracles
- The prophecies and their fulfillment
  - Simply look at the Jesus Prophesies and Fulfillment theme scripture sheet in HYB/

Mods for 50 prophecies fulfilled there alone.

- Lack of any explanation for Earth's creation other than God

The Doctrine of God

- "God is a spirit" Jhn 4:24
    - As a spirit He can reveal Himself as He likes, eg: as Jesus in John 1:18
- "God is Love" 1 Jn 4:8
    - This Love is also supported in His character as Righteous, Merciful, and Goodness. It is not to say that if someone has love they have God.
- He has Characteristics:
    - Aseity - "Neither is worshiped with men's hands, as though he needed any thing" Acts 17:25
    - Goodness - Romans 11:22 i
    - "Merciful and gracious, long-suffering, and abundant in goodness and truth" Exodus 34:5-6
    - Holy - Isaiah 6:3 , Revelation 4:8

- Immutability, that means God cannot change - James 1:17
- Omnipotence = "all powerful" - Matthew 19:26
- Omnipresence = being present everywhere Psalm 139:8
- Omniscience of God refers to him being "all knowing" Romans 16:27
- God is One (see a much longer list of these written out in the Themes chapter in HYB/ Mods)

Deuteronomy 4:35, Deuteronomy 6:4, II Sam. 7:22, I Chronicles 17:20, Psalm 86:10, Isaiah 44:6, Isaiah 45:5-6, Zechariah 14:9, Matthew 1:23, Mark 12:29, John 8:56-59, John 14:6-7, I Corinthians 8:4-6, I Timothy 2:5, James 2:19, Revelations 4:2, Revelations 22:13

The Identity of Jesus

- Wholly God, leaving nothing out Col 2:9, 2 Cor 5:19
- The one you must believe in to be saved Jn 8:24
- The “I am” of the OT Jn 8:58
- “God” Jn 20:28, Hebrews 1:8

- "Lord" Acts 9:5
- "Jehovah" Is 45:23 + Phil 2:10-11
- "Father" Is 9:6, Rev 21:6-7
- "Word" Jn 1:14
- "Holy Spirit" Jn 14:17-18

*Note: there is no room for another "person(s)" to be identified, Jesus is the embodiment of all of the titles given to God

- Both God and the Lamb Rev 22:3-4
- Son of God Luke 1:35, Gal 4:4, Heb 1:5 (not to say "God the Son," that phrase is not found in the Bible)
    - This refers to Jesus' humanity and His nature as a man, in unity with His identity as God. God did not stop being the Creator or Father, and was still a spirit, just as Jesus now. "Son of God" is very well translated "Made of God" or "from God," which is consistent with the scripture John 1:14 and 1 Timothy 3:16,
- He was Human
    - He was born Mt 1:20-25
    - He thirsted Jhn 19:28
    - He ate 1 Cr 11:23

  - He died 1 Th 4:14

Angels and Demons

- They were both created, just like everything else, by God Gen 1:1, Acts 14:15, Rev 4:11
- Believers in Christ have the power of angles James 4:7 , 1 Jn 4:4
- Demons are actually angels that have fallen Mat 25:41
- Christians have the power to cast out and remove devils/ demons Mark 6:13, 16:17
- The Devil was known as Lucifer and was once in Heaven Isaiah 14:12–15

Humanity

- We are created in the image of God Gen 1:27
- We have a propensity to sin, born out of a selfish nature, and can not escape sin on our own Psalm 51:5, 58:3, Rom 3:9
- This sin came into the world through Adam and Eve Genesis 3:14-19, Rom 5:14
- None are right with God on their own Rom 3:10 , Rom 3:23

Jesus' work in Salvation

- Sins are purged by sacrifice Lev 4:26, Heb 9:22
- The sacrifice of animals was not sufficient

  Heb 10:4
- Jesus came as a perfect sacrifice Rom 3:24-25
- There is no salvation outside of this sacrifice, Jesus Jn 14:6 Jn 8:24
- The Bible gives several complementary descriptions of Jesus'' death
  - "Redemption" Gal 3:13
  - "Ransom" Mat 20:28 1 Tim 2:6
  - "Propitiation" (this means appeasement)

    Rom 3:25 1 Jn 2:2
  - "Reconciliation" Rom 5:6-11 2 Cor 5:14-21
  - "Substitution" Is 53:5-6 2 Cor 5:21
- After He was sacrificed He was buried, and conquered Hell/Hades Acts 2:25-32

- He raised again victorious over death
  Rom 4:25 1 Cor 15:14

Elements of Salvation

- Everyone's need for salvation Rom 3:9-12 , Rom 3:23 , 1 Jn 1:8-10
- Faith Eph 2:8-9

This means that we apply the grace God offers through Faith

- The Gospel 1 Cor 15:1-4

* These earlier three bring the following 3:

- Repentance 2 Pet 3:9 , Mark 1:15 ,
  - Includes Confession of Sin Mark 2:17
  - Sorrow for Sin 2 Cor 7:10
  - and a Decision against sinning Rom 6:1
- Water Baptism Rom 6:1-5 , 1 Pet 3:21 , Mark 16:16 , Acts 2:41
- It's important to note that no one was ever sprinkled or poured over, in baptism. Look at the End Resources Baptism Theme scripture sheet, everywhere a mode is offered it is in submersion, and that is the meaning of "baptism" in Greek. Also, in every time a

"formula" was noted, in a baptism Jesus name was used. Never was a person baptized in the Bible under titles like father or uncle. 1 Cor 1:13, 6:11, Gal 3:27, Col 2:12,

- Infilling of the Holy Ghost Is 28:11-12 , Acts 2:38 , John 3:5 , Rom 8:1-16 , 1 Cor 12:13 , Eph 1:13-14 , Titus 3:5 , Mark 16:17
    - No only for elite Christians or specially gifted people, this is needed to be saved by everyone John 7:38-39 , Acts 5:32 , 11:15-17 , 19:2 , Galatians 3:14 , Eph 1:13
    - 5 specific accounts of Holy Ghost infilling are recorded with distinct people
        - Jews Acts 2:4
            - Tongues recorded
        - Samaritans Acts 8:17
            - Tongues implied in this passage, as Simon wanted the supernatural power to deliver the Holy Ghost and it's signs
        - Gentiles Acts 10:44-46
            - Tongues recorded. Notice that this sign is enough for the Jews to understand they had received the

same Holy Ghost

- Paul Acts 9:17-18
    - Tongues not recorded here, but in 1 Cor 14:18
- John's disciples Acts 19:6
    - Tongues recorded as the first sign

Christian Living

- Nothing outside the Christian can separate us from salvation Rom 8:35-39
- Christians can leave their salvation
- Rom 11:17-23 , Heb 2:1-4
- There is a Christian lifestyle Titus 2:11-12
- Freedom shouldn't be abused 1 Cor 6:12
- Elements of a Christian Lifestyle
    - Prayer Jude 1:20-21 , Mat 6:5-15 , Eph 6:18
    - Bible Study 2 Tim 2:15 , 3:14-17
    - Faithful Church Attendance Heb 10:25
    - Giving Tithes and Offerings Malachi 3:8-12 , Luke 6:38 , 16:10-12 , 1 Cor 9:7-14

  - Worship of God in order Psalm 100:1-5 , 1 Cor 14:26-33 , Eph 5:19-20
  - Fasting Mat 6:16-18
  - Holiness Heb 12:14 , 1 Pet 1:15-16 , Rom 12:1-2
    - This means conforming to God's character, and leaving our selfish nature. It includes separation and dedication.
  - Sexual purity 1 Cor 6:9
- Appearance
  - Distinction of the sexes in dress Deut 22:5
  - Distinction of the sexes in hair length 1 Cor 11:1-6
  - Modesty in dress 1 Tim 2:8-10
  - Rejection of adornment 1 Pet 3:1-5
- Sanctity of Human life (includes suicide and abortion) Jer 1:5 , Zech 12:1 , Mat 5:21
- Honesty Mark 10:19

(Notes)

____

____

//Reading plans//

Here are 7 reading plans, described and ready for your use. With one of them you can read the Bible in 3 months! There are a lot of options that are available to you. Reading the Bible in time-line (chronological) order is also a good option. You might opt for a slower one-year reading of the Bible, mixing Old Testament with new, or straight through cover to cover. All of these reading plans are available to you. Many are PDF format so you can print, cut, and glue them right into your Bible or journal!

People often buy special "reading plan Bibles" to keep at their night stand for $20-$80; take these resources and use them free in HYB/ Apps! I hope you find this book to be a great value.

www.BiblePlan.org

This is a great site that's just a little bit ugly. They have an abundance of translations, and their Bible studies are emailed to your inbox daily.

This service is a great exercise for many, I think, to make Bible study a part of your work day. Many professionals are already checking their email daily and could use some morning faith building.

52 Week Bible Reading Plan

This is a little different, and if you've read the Bible through a few times you might think consider this new approach.

Each day of the week is a different part of the Bible, like Psalms for Wednesdays and the Gospels on Sat. I would usually worry about losing the scripture's context skipping around, but this plan has you reading chapters at a time, not just a smattering of verses. Find the printable PDF here[9].

My-Bible-Plans

With this site[10] you can custom build a great Bible reading plan. Include whatever books of the Bible you like, set the time-line however long you want and starting whatever date you want. This is especially nice if you're starting mid-year; you won't have to play "catch up."

You can read the Bible right there in your browser

---

9 http://www.bible-reading.com/bible-plan.pdf

10 http://www.mybibleplans.com/

like it's a blog post. Alongside the scriptures to read are audio versions so you can read and hear it at the same time. They will even email you your passage if you like, daily.

The downsides are that you can't print the plan, and the only Bible version to be delivered is ESV. These limitations are game-enders for me, but maybe not you.

Bible Reading Chart: Here[11]

This is a beautiful chart that allows you to mark off your reading and see the progression. You'll likely want to pair this with another reading plan to set your own pace (open it and you'll understand, there's not dates.)

The visual momentum this chart creates is important to first time Bible readers. In many large projects (like reading the greatest book in history) excitement or responsibility will start you off strong but the fear of losing all the work you've already done will help you finish.

So if you have half the chart marked off, and don't feel like you can read today- you will so that

[11] http://visualunit.files.wordpress.com/2010/12/bible_reading.pdf

you don't lose all the progress made.

An added bonus is that there aren't any dates on this chart, so if you reading bridges over a new year, or starts late, it's no big deal.

5x5x5 Plan

Printable here[12]. This is what they write about the plan:

"5 minutes a day | If you're not currently reading the Bible, start with 5 minutes a day. This reading plan will take you through all 260 chapters of the New Testament, one chapter per day. The gospels are read throughout the year to keep the story of Jesus fresh all year.

5 days a week | Determine a time and location to spend 5 minutes a day for 5 days a week. It is best to have a consistent time and a quiet place where you can regularly meet with the Lord.

5 ways to dig deeper | We must pause in our reading to dig into the Bible. Below are 5 different ways to dig deeper each day. These exercises will encourage meditation. We recommend trying a

---

[12] http://www.navpress.com/uploadedFiles/5x5x5_BRP.pdf

single idea for a week to find what works best for you."

Remember to keep a pen and journal ready to capture insights.

1. Underline or highlight key words or phrases in the Bible passage. Use a pen or highlighter to mark new discoveries from the text. Periodically review your

markings to see what God is teaching you.

2. Put it into your own words. Read the passage or verse slowly, then rewrite

each phrase or sentence using your own words.

3. Ask and answer some questions. Questions unlock new discoveries and

meanings. Ask questions about the passage using these words: who, what, why,

when, where, or how. Jot down some thoughts on how you would answer

these questions.

4. Capture the big idea. God's Word communicates big ideas. Periodically ask,

What's the big idea in this sentence, paragraph, or chapter?

5. Personalize the meaning. When God speaks to us through the Scriptures, we must respond. A

helpful habit is personalizing the Bible through application. Ask: How could my life be different today as I respond to what I'm reading?"

The only downside to this reading plan is that it only plans for the New Testament. I might adapt my own version of this sheet for the entire Bible, but until then use this to get the most you can out of your NT reading.

Straight Through Bible Reading Plan

This chart is ready for you to print, fold, and put in the back of your Bible if you just get the email packet. Depending on the year that you receive this book the dates might not line up perfectly. You can either search for a new version online, contact me at HackYourBible.com, or ask your pastor for one. The plan is found at the back of this guide ready to use. Maybe couple this chart with the beautiful Bible Reading Chart from before[13].

---

13 http://visualunit.files.wordpress.com/2010/12/bible_reading.pdf

Chronological Bible Reading Plan

If you want to read the story of the Bible, in the order that it happened, then here is a plan formatted for you. It's an adaptation from others, and I have to confess that there will always be controversy over what order is correct. This is as close as I can come right now It's interesting to read it this way though. You get to read the Bible a little more like a novel. This is available at the end of the book.

This Book is incomplete

Get the rest here:

- Printable End Resources
- Kid's Hacks
- Shareable Version of HYB
- Workshop Hand Outs/ Helps
- Video Demos

Go to http://eepurl.com/GHH_T

or scan this QR code:

Sign up and we'll put the freebies in your email inbox immediately!

//Free commentaries//

Commentaries are books of comments on the scriptures. These comments may include historical insight, cross referencing, or application. There are many commentaries available online for free. Often what you pay is the value you receive. The best resource of free ones I know of are on BLB.org. There are also many commentaries that are very good, that you would usually pay for, that you can get from libraries both public and at universities.

*A serious note on commentaries:

It takes a mature mind to entertain an idea and not accept it.

Go back and read that again.

If you read outside the influence of your own doctrine, you must eat what little meat is there and must spit out the bones; they could kill you. Non-critical reading, and not checking what one is reading with spiritual authority, is THE leading reason for Christians losing their faith. I've lost dear friends this exact way.

That said, and I hope you really understood that,

there is a little value in seeing how others have interpreted the Bible. If for no other reason than to take better aim at their false doctrine. At present I do not know of any complete commentaries compiled at the PHD level within the Apostolic movement. If you know of one, or want to offer other good commentaries to the Bible hacker community, just contact me at www.HackYourBible.com

Sometimes what the other guys write has insight for our own lives, but we must always stop and think about how accepting their idea affects the rest of our understanding. An example: if Genesis is just an analogy, or poem, and maybe the flood was just local to Noah's area... then God is a liar, and is not all powerful or righteous.

Little neat ideas have a way of undermining pillars of faith. Be careful. Be in conversation with your pastor. Be in constant prayer. This stuff matters.

//Key Sheets//

These Key Sheets are great tools for outreach or even in small group study. Inform yourself on the religious systems these people you are trying to reach are in. There are reasons they subscribe to these doctrines, and there are weaknesses in them they don't yet see.

You can be on better-than-even terms with Atheists, Catholics, Baptists, and Muslims with these quick, small pages to include in your Bible. How will you defend the Bible's authority? Or reconcile science and the Bible? Or refute evolution as man's source rather than God? Key sheets, that's how.

I thought about making these a separate product, and charging $15 because of the work involved in crafting them, but decided to include them in the HYB+ package. I hope you use them!

Muslims

About:

The 2nd fastest growing religion next to Pentecostalism. They believe in the Quran, and the Hadiths (Histories) for context on the Quran. They believe that both are Infallible. (see " Is The Qur'an the Word of God?"[14] online for a deep study of why this is wrong)

Differences:

- Believe Mohammed was a prophet, because of Quran; believe in the Quran because of Mohammed (circular logic)
- They say Bible changed often, but Quran is pure (See Essential Bible Doctrines earlier in this book)
- Believe that the Quran is God's (Allah's) word, literally written through men and not inspired and written by men. Then it was checked by Mohammed for accuracy. However the Hadith speak of the Quran being compiled later than Mohammed, because Zayd ibn Thabit fears the wars would cause sections to be lost. (ie: it wasn't compiled yet) So it was not checked my Mohamed.
- Different historical copies: Ubi-ibn-Kab's in Syria had 116 chapters (today's has 114), Ibn-Masoud's had only 111
- Hadith records Uthman sending out his copy of the Quran and ordering anything different

---

[14] http://www.answering-islam.org/Resources/Morey/quran.html

burned. Why the purge?

- They believe that you must read Arabic to understand the Quran wholly.

Similarities:

- Believe in one God (this is their greatest contention with Trinitarian Christianity)
- Believe Jesus was a historical figure
- Believe on Moses and Abraham

Thoughts for Muslims:

- Does the Quran know History or Science? (read why not Here[15])
- Does the Quran agree with itself? Is it internally consistent? (read why not Here[16])
- Why is SO much of the Quran plagiarized? (See Muhammad's Plagiarism[17])
- Why is the Quran disorganized and scattered, if it is one revelation from one God?

---

15 http://www.answering-islam.org/Quran/Contra/#external

16 http://www.answering-islam.org/Quran/Contra/#internal

17 http://wikiislam.net/wiki/Muhammads_Plagiarism

Southern Baptist Convention

About:

This is the largest group of Baptists, and is also the most conservative arm. Akin to us as "sons of the reformation" they are supposed to believe in scripture above all else, and are against most of the traditions of the Catholics.

Differences + Contrary Scriptures:

- Baptism is just a symbol of faith (Rom 6:1-5, 1 Pet 3:21, Mark 16:16, Acts 2:41)
- Trinity (See the Oneness Theme in HYB+ or the Essential Bible Doctrines Summary for many scriptures)
- Total Depravity (or Inability to choose good) *Very important point* - They say "we all are sinful or corrupted and damned from birth; so depraved we can't even choose anything good, including God's salvation, without God making us choose" This is not Biblical. (Rom 5, 1 Cor 15 say nothing of this doctrine, nor Gen 1) Also, the Biblical demand that we "choose salvation" is in conflict with this doctrine (Josh 24:15, Acts 2:40 Paul "exhorts" Jews to do the impossible? Acts 17:30 can we repent? Rom 1 says "without excuse") God

did not exact impossible demands on His people.

- Unconditional Election - God elects people to be saved and they have no say (Josh 24:15, Acts 2:40, Acts 17:30)
- Limited Atonement - Jesus did not die for the people that are not elected, and they can not be saved despite their pursuit or love of God (Eze 18:23, 1 Jn 2:2, 2 Cor 5:15, Heb 2:9)
- Irresistible Grace - The people God elects are saved regardless if they want to be (2 Pet 2:1-2 , Jer 4:4,)
- Perseverance of the Saints - Once saved you can not leave, ever. No matter your actions you can not lose salvation (Jn 15:5-6, Col 1:22-23, Heb 10:28-29)

Similarities:

- Often baptize through immersion instead of sprinkling or pouring
- Generally oppose infant baptism
- Conservatives (SBC) believe the Bible is inspired, liberals (General "Baptist" or "Reformed") you'll have to defend the Bible first with
- Priesthood of all believers - everyone has the

right to minister to others

- "Soul Competency" each person is their own before God, no inherited faith/salvation
- Thoughts for them:
- Talk about the inspiration of the whole Bible, and ask if all of it should be used
- Compare the exclusive doctrine to Jehovah Witnesses
- Get them out of commentaries and into the Bible

Methodists

About:

Founded in 1968, traces to the John and Charles Wesley "Holiness" movement. 2nd largest Protestant group after Southern Baptist Convention. In 2007 had 12million members.

Differences:

- Bishop based power structure, sees itself as part Catholic
- Trinity (See the Oneness Theme in HYB+ or the Essential Bible Doctrines Summary for many scriptures)
- Baptism is just a symbol of faith, done by sprinkling, pouring, or immersion (Rom 6:1-5,

1 Pet 3:21, Mark 16:16, Acts 2:41) Done in the Trinity (1 Cor 1:13, 6:11, Gal 3:27, Col 2:12)

- Sinner's Prayer can bring grace and salvation alone (Acts 2:38, James 2:18,20,26)[18]

Similarities:

- Believe in free Will (not like Baptists)
- Rejects “Eternal Security” or “once saved always saved”
- Originally believed Holiness lifestyle
- Originally believed in the Holy Ghost and miracles
- Believe the Bible is inspired by God, though often do not read it literally
- Salvation through Jesus alone
- Jesus Died and by Him we receive salvation

Thoughts for them:

- Once we were the same, why did you change?
- If it was important to your founder, what changed since?

---

[18] See Essential Bible Doctrines in HYB: Elements of salvation

- Has that change been good?

Atheists/ Agnostics

About

First you must know that Atheists and Agnostics are making a faith-claim. They are not simply "without faith," or not believers; they do believe something. They have to prove their just as much as we do. Atheists are saying that there is no God. Agnostics say that we can not know God. You should press them on this. Force them to prove their point, do not get stuck on defense.

Differences - Atheists, they say:

- "There is no God" - any idea of him was man made to explain phenomenon
- God does not matter, as He is unprovable
- Religion is a disease that leads to evil / suffering and should be eradicated

Proofs against their faith-claims:

1. Without God you lose a Uniformity of Humanity (evolution demands that all of humanity is not equal) and Human Dignity (man is the same as animals)
2. You also lose Universal morals, and what

is "right". Only 2 options for an Atheist's morals: (And these are not necessarily reasons for universal adherence)

- Social Contract / Mutual Benefit - Then what about Nazi's? Was that not evil? If I can convince our society that we deserve to split all of your things and kill you, does that make it "right?"
- Individual/ Personal Benefit, aka "what works best for me" - How do you know what is best for you? You haven't seen the future; so you have no basis for "right." And, what if I decide that to steal all your things, is that OK if I decide that is what is right for me?

3. Creates a Despair of Meaning - Our lives are worthless in the scheme of things, if there is not a God that values us and preserves our essence after an Earthly life. Without God we are all accidents waiting to disappear.
4. Love must then be an abstraction of lust and the need to procreate, and "true love" is a figment of the imagination. There should never have been

monogamy; it's counter productive.

5. Atheism is foundational to evil

    - All of the Inquisition, Middle East conflicts, and the Holy Wars combined don't amount to one of the atrocities committed by Adolf Hitler, Joseph Stalin, or Mao Zedong in the pursuit of a religion-free utopia (source Here[19], more Here[20])

    - The holocaust was made possible by an atheistic view, and the inclusion of evolution. Nazi view: Jews are less evolved, therefore more animal, and allowed to be exterminated. There is not a God that opposes this.

Differences - Agnostics say:

- "There may be a God, but there is absolutely no way to prove it"
    - See earlier proof against Atheism
- Because we can't prove God, we can't know what He wants from us

---

19 http://www.csmonitor.com/2006/1121/p09s01-coop.html

20 http://scholarscorner.com/apologia/deathtoll.html

  - These people are functionally atheists, usually without conviction enough to declare themselves a full atheist
  - See Essential Bible Doctrines : The Bible, for support for the Bible as the word of God.

Similarities:

- Believe that real Christianity shouldn't be a business, or power grab
- They reject the Trinity
- They reject Islam as a plague on the Earth

Talking Points:

- Is denying God worth losing all of your inalienable rights?
- Why is this person actively excluding the possibility of a God that cares about them? Often it is a desire to be self ruled, no matter the consequences.
- What other reasons for creation are there? Evolution? (See Evolution Key Sheet)
- How are there universal Laws of Nature, if there is not a uniform source or Law Giver?
- Why can we eat our "brother-in-accident" the cow, or soy bean, but not our brother

Evander Holyfield? Why is cannibalism "wrong" and not just unhealthy?

Evolution/ Science

Things they say, and Christian responses

- The universe happened without a Creator
    - The fact that there are uniform "Laws of the Universe" demands a "Law Giver." Otherwise, why are there not substances that gravity doesn't affect? Aren't these laws necessary for creation to continue?
- "Time + Chance = Everything" In example this sounds like: "if you had a million apes on a million typewriters they would eventually type the complete works of Shakespeare."
    - Math disagrees. This is called the Gambler's Fallacy[21]: the false idea that as a bet is repeated over time the odds improve.
        - After a "heads" on a coin flip there is not a better chance that the next flip will produce "tails." Time does not

---

21 http://en.wikipedia.org/wiki/Gambler's_fallacy

improve chance. To think so is to not understand math.

- Physics disagrees. The 2nd Law of Thermodynamics is simply "the entropy (spread and disorder of energy) of the universe increases every time energy is used, or a reaction occurs." You've experienced this, a ball rolling always stops. Because we can test and time this destruction of energy/mass, we know that there is not enough time for evolution to have happened. (This is per Andrew McIntosh, as Professor of Thermodynamics at Leeds.) More Here[22].

- Simple things changed, and as the changes were an advantage they were reproduced and took over the species, or changed the species. This is the explanation of the origin of our complex lifeforms.
    - Biology disagrees. The Law of Irreducible Complexity proves that there are systems in life, like blood clotting, that if you try to make them more simple (proving

---

22 http://www.seekfind.net/_The_Age_Of_The_Earth_Is_Not_A_Factor_Because_Of_The_Second_Law_Of_Thermodynamics_Which_Is_The_Law_Of_Entropy.html–

evolution right by showing their previous step) they fail. And everything dies. (further reading Here[23])

Suggested Talking Points

- "Please explain the Big Bang, what was there in the beginning?" Once they give you their 3-5 things ask "You mean that ____ and ____ and (whatever else) eventually combined to give us sadness, and hope, and love? That our greatest ambitions are made of these things?" (via Dustin Morre)
- Why are there uniform Laws in the universe?
- Micro-evolution does not prove Macro-evolution (birds may grow to have more advantageous beaks, but they won't become frogs. Species may change within themselves, but do not become new species)
- How did the inanimate (dirt) become animate (bacteria)? Has that ever been replicated, or witnessed?

---

23 http://www.amazon.com/Darwins-Black-Box-Biochemical-Challenge/dp/0743290313

Roman Catholic Church

About:

1 of 6 Americans are Catholic, and there are 1 Billion in the world. This is the largest Christian denomination in the world.

Differences and responses:

- They claim to be "Apostolic" through succession (bishop to bishop) not doctrine
    - No Biblical evidence that Peter was bishop of Rome, or first Pope
    - Irenaeus, the early bishop 178-200 AD, provided list of 1st 12 bishops of Rome. He did not include Peter, and says 1st Bishop of Rome was Linus
    - Eusebius, the "father of church history" c.260 to <341, never mentions Peter as Bishop of Rome
    - Paul, in the book Romans, greets 24+ people in Rome, but never Peter
- Purgatory (Not a doctrine in the Bible, 2 Cor 5:8, Phil 1:21-23)
- Praying to the saints and Mary (1 Tim 2:5, Phil 4:6, Mat 6:9)
- That Mary was sinless like Jesus (Lk 1:46 - She

needs salvation too, Mk 10:18, Lk 2:22-24 Mary's sin offering)

- They include the Apocrypha in their Bible.
    - Apocrypha has many errors of Biology, History, Geography, and Chronology. It also conflicts with itself often in Theology
    - The 1st Century Church never accepted it
    - Contains no prophesy to help substantiate it
    - Contains many non-Biblical doctrines, in conflict with the established Bible
    - Catholics didn't include it until 1546, to combat the Reformation
    - Never claims to be of God
- Authority of Church tradition (Mat 15:1-9, Col 2:8-10)

Similarities:

- Believe the God of Abraham, Isaac, and Jacob is the creator
- Jesus was born of a Virgin, lived sinless, died, and raised as in the Bible, and is coming again to judge mankind
- There will be a future resurrection

- Old Testament and New Testament are inspired, infallible word of God
- We love Mary too, for being willing to carry Jesus
    - Talking point: ... and she got the Holy Ghost, too, like you should!

Talking Points:

- Why are there so many factions of Catholics, if they have the truth? (eg: Vatican 1, Vatican 2, to name 2 of the 242[24] factions)
- Challenge them to read the New Testament in the next 3 months, and highlight all the references to Purgatory, Praying to Mary, Praying to the Dead, and References to the Apocrypha. Regroup at three months and discuss what they've found.
- Which is more important: the Apostle's doctrine, or the traditions of an organization? If it is the doctrine then let's start a Bible study from the Apostle's book!

---

[24] The Oxford World Christian Encyclopedia

Mormons

About:

The mass majority of converts to Mormonism were Christian before. They use "Christian-speak" to confuse weak Christians. Very family focused and are for most traditional values.

Similarities:

- They refuse to drink alcohol
- Are proponents of traditional marriage

Talking points:

- The Bible says Jesus is God, Mormons say He "became a God" for his good works
- They say Elohim makes spirit babies with a goddess wife, that need a body from us procreating. This contradicts the Bible (Mat 19:2, Deu 4:35, I Ch 17:20, Isa 44:6)
- "You wouldn't call Jesus a demi-god would you?" or "Would you compare Jesus and Satan?" Their answer: No, never.
    - Their holy book says that Elohim had two sons: Jesus and Lucifer, and that they fought over who would save Adam and Even.
- Why would the Bible say "But though we, or an angel from heaven, preach any other

gospel unto you than that which we have preached unto you, let him be accursed." Gal 1:8 (Their revelation from the angel Moroni? Comparable to Islam's origin from an "angel")

- More: Banned Mormon Cartoon[25] video - does this seem "the same as Christian"?

Jehovah Witnesses

About:

95% of converts to JW were Christian before. They use "Christian-speak" to confuse weak Christians. Once in a Watchtower study group of the they work to isolate the prospect from other friends. They report 18 million adherents.

Talking Points:

- Why do they believe that Jesus is the archangel Michael? (Page 393 of "Insight on the Scriptures") The Bible never says this
    - Heb 1:4 says Jesus is "better than the angels," in v.6 the angels worship Him
- They will ask "Are you worried about current events?" Answer: no, I have the peace of God

25 http://www.youtube.com/watch?v=n3BqLZ8UoZk

- They talk about the "coming Kingdom."
  - Answer: are you still waiting?
  - Lk 17:20-21 - Kingdom is here!
  - Rom 14:17 - It is: "righteousness, and peace, and joy in the Holy Ghost"
- How can anyone use a translation from a man without any Greek background?
  - Kingdom interlinear translation is not a translation, but a poor commentary. Don't accept this in a Bible study.
- If the name Jehovah is so important, then why is it never used in the entire Greek New Testament? (Acts 4:12)
- Read Deu 18:20-22 - Concerning the many failed predictions of the Watchtower, claiming to be a "prophetic" book.
- More: Questions for Jehovah's Witnesses[26]

[26] http://carm.org/questions-for-jehovahs-witnesses

// Bible Studies to build into Bible//

There are a lot of Bible studies, on a lot of subjects out there. These I've formatted, again, for you to use as a Built in Chain Reference Bible Study. You can find instructions on how to build these scriptures into your Bible in HYB/Mods for instant access.

I'm not saying I did all the research, a lot of these were already written and free online, and I just verified them. You could do this work on your own, or just get them here with all the other resources. How much was the last Bible study you saw for sale? How about 5 of them, freely included, just for you?

Subjects covered are:

- 1Hr to salvation - for getting them to a decision now, not later
- Who or What is Jesus?
- Baptisms in the Bible, and what they tell us
- Is the Holy Ghost important? Is it always proved by "speaking in tongues?"
- What a Christian should live like

1Hr to salvation - for getting them to a decision now, not later

Many Bible Studies don't get to the heart of the matter soon enough. This is a modification of my friend Art Farmer's Bible study. It was originally a two hour, two session Bible study that he used with great success. 60+ people were baptized in about a year with him delivering the study alone.

Follow the directions in HYB/Mods chapter "The Built in 'Chain Bible Study." Here you're given a list of scriptures in a certain order to draw a square around and reference forward in progression. There is also a little note on what the verse says, if you don't think you could explain just by reading it.

Always pray before Bible studies!

- Luke 21:33-34 - The Bible is still relevant, and we don't want to be caught "unawares"
- Matt 24:24 - There will be a fake "Christianity" they will be tricky
- Matt 7:14 - It's not an open and easy thing to get to heaven; not "just do good"
- Matt 7:21- "Good Christians" are going to go to Hell, we don't want to be one of them
- Matt 22:10 - We can't come our own way,

the parable says

- Jude 1:1 - The first way is still the best way, only 38 yrs after Jesus there's confusion
- Gal 1:6-9 - "Accursed" means "damned forever," changing salvation is a big deal
- John 3:3-5 - "born again" or no heaven - what is this "water and Spirit"?
- Matt 16:18 - What are those keys? And who was the rock? Unstable Peter? no, Jesus
- Matt 28:18-20 - Which is a name: Jesus, Son, Father, or Spirit?
- Ex 6:3 - Old Testament name is JEHOVAH
- Matt 1:21 - Jesus = "Jehovah is salvation"
- Luke 13:3 - First Key: Repentance *Jesus' words
- Mark 16:15-20 - Second Key: Baptism *Jesus' words
- Luke 24:44-49 - Third Key: Holy Ghost (promised here) *Jesus' words
- Acts 1:5,8,15 - Preparing for the first Holy Ghost experience
- Acts 2:1-17 - first Holy Ghost experience/ what the Holy Ghost looks like
- Joel 2:28 - Prophecy of Joel about Holy Ghost

- Acts 2:36-42 - Peter uses the keys
- Acts 8:5 - Proof of the Spirit in Philip + More Holy ghost
- Acts 10:40-48 - Peter using the Keys with non-Jews
- Acts 19:1-6 - Re-baptism and more Holy Ghost in the early church
- Mark 16:16 - Need for Baptism again
- Matt 7:13-14,21 - We need to follow the Bible way
- Acts 22:16 - ...and what is "the name of the Lord"?
- Acts 9:5, 17-18 - Jesus = the name of the Lord
- Acts 4:10-12 - No salvation outside of Jesus' name
- Gal 3:26-27 - Not into the "father, son, holy ghost" but Jesus
- Colo 3:17 - If you do anything, do it in Jesus name; even baptism
- Colo 2:8-12 - Baptizing in the titles might me traditional some places, but the Bible says to do it in Jesus name. Don't be caught up in "vain deceits"
- John 7:37-39 - Jesus was talking about the Holy Ghost, and how it was from Jesus

- Eph 4:4-6 - 1 Lord (Jesus)= 1 Faith (in Jesus)= 1 Baptism (in Jesus name)
- James 1:21-22 - Knowing isn't enough
- Heb 5:8-9 - We have to Obey
- Luke 6:46-49 - Do the Word and have a strong foundation

Who or What is Jesus?

There is already a Theme for this under :Mods: but if you want a good, step by step Bible study disproving the Trinity here you go.

Follow the directions in HYB/Mods chapter "The Built in 'Chain Bible Study." Here you're given a list of scriptures in a certain order to draw a square around and reference forward in progression. There is also a little note on what the verse says, if you don't think you could explain just by reading it.

Always pray before Bible studies.

- Mat 28:18-19 - The one with all 88power speaks of His own name, declaring titles of power
- Deuteronomy 6:4 - Early declaration of God's Identity
- Isaiah 44:8 & 24 - God was the creator and redeemer alone, not as a panel
- Isaiah 45:5-6 - Specifically states there's is no "other person" or God beside Him
- Isaiah 43:10-11 - Not only no other eternal God, but none made after
- Isaiah 9:6 - Jesus = God

- Matthew 1:23 - Jesus' identity = God with us, not a demigod or other person
- John 1:1,14 - "Word" is not an eternal Jesus, but God's will and wants
- John 17:3 - Only one true God
- John 20:28 - Was Thomas wrong, did he not Know Jesus?
- John 20:29 - No, Jesus affirms his revelation
- 1st Timothy 2:5 - Does this mean the all powerful God has to rely on Jesus?
- John 10:30
- John 8:24 & 27 - Jesus is the Father, not just a representation of Him or an agent
- John 5:7 - Even the Holy Ghost is included in Jesus, because all are God - All verses that talk about God, or The Father, or the Creator point to one God. Every last one of them are surrounded in modifiers in their original language who's context means exclusively one. (ie: Those Sheep, or That Sheep. The latter means exclusively one) Over 2,000 of these mentions point to one God.
- Colossians 2:9 - Jesus encompasses all of the

Godhead, not that He is a part of it[27]

- Jehovah means Lord. Most times in the Old Testament it was coupled with an attribute of God, a piece of His character. Jesus also meets all of these characteristics
- Jehovah-jireh
  - Genesis 22:14 The Lord will provide
- Jehovah-rapha
  - Exodus 15:26 The Lord that heals
- Jehovah-nissi
  - Exodus 17:15 The Lord our victory
- Jehovah-m'kaddesh
  - Exodus 31:13 The Lord that sanctifies
- Jehovah-shalom
  - Judges 6:24 The Lord our peace
- Jehovah-saboath
  - 1st Samuel 1:3 The Lord Almighty
- Jehovah-elyon
  - Psalm 7:17 The Lord most high

---

[27] For more information on the Oneness of the Godhead, read "The Oneness of God" by David K. Bernard.

- Jehovah-raah
    - Psalm 23:1 The Lord my shepherd
- Jehovah-hossenu
    - Psalm 95:6 The Lord our maker
- Jehovah-tsidkenu
    - Jeremiah 23:6 The Lord our righteousness
- Jehovah-Savior
    - Matthew 1:21 Jesus
- Genesis 1:26 - "And God said, Let us make man in our image." Possibly speaking to self, like “let’s see...”, or there was more than one image, ie: angels.
- Genesis 1:27 -Singular again, both the image created in and the creator

Baptisms in the Bible, and what they tell us

There is already a Theme for this subject in the book "Hack Your Bible/ Mods" but if you want a good, step by step Bible study disproving the Trinitarian baptism formula here you go. I understand if you don't feel qualified to just start pointing out scriptures.

Follow the directions in HYB/Mods chapter "The Built in 'Chain Bible Study." Here you're given a list of scriptures in a certain order to draw a square around and reference forward in progression. There is also a little note on this sheet what the verse is about, if you don't think you could explain just by reading it. Always pray before Bible studies!

Write this as a note at the head of the scripture series:

"Baptism is from (Greek) baptizō verb :

1) to dip repeatedly, to immerse, to submerge (of vessels sunk)

2) to cleanse by dipping or submerging, to wash, to make clean with water, to wash one's self, bathe

3) to overwhelm

(From the Strong's Concordance with Hebrew and Greek Lexicon) "

- Matthew 28:18-19 - The one with all power speaks of His own name, declaring His titles of power
- Mark 16:15-16 - Baptism is a must to get to Heaven
- John 3:5 - Jesus says that Baptism is a must to get to Heaven
- Luke 24:47 - It's all in Jesus name, baptism and your salvation
- Acts 2:38 - Peter gives a method "in Jesus name" and a promise of the Holy Ghost
- Acts 2:41 - The people, in the Bible, do just what Peter just said
- Acts 9:18 - Paul's Baptism was immediately after he heard about it
- Acts 10:47-48 - Baptism can not be restrained, it must be done
- Acts 18:8 - If you believe, then you will be baptized
- James 2:26 - Show your faith is alive
- Acts 19:3-5 - An example of people being re-baptized, into the name of Jesus

- Acts 22:16 - Call on the name of the Lord (Jesus) and don't wait being baptized
- Ephesians 4:5 - 1 Lord (Jesus)= 1 Faith (in Jesus)= 1 Baptism (in Jesus name)

* End with "are you ready to be baptized?"

Always have a local place available where you can baptize a person, even if it's just a local pastor you can call for the church to be opened. I would not wait for their family to interrupt or confuse them; unless they are under age and there may be a legal issue.

Is the Holy Ghost important? Is it always proved by "speaking in tongues?"

There is already a Theme for this subject in the book "Hack Your Bible/ Mods" but if you want a good, step by step Bible study proving the need for the Holy Ghost, and that it comes with speaking in tongues here you go. I understand if you don't feel qualified to just start pointing out scriptures.

Follow the directions in HYB/Mods chapter "The Built in 'Chain Bible Study." Here you're given a list of scriptures in a certain order to draw a square around and reference forward in progression. There is also a little note on this sheet what the verse is about, to copy next to the verse if you don't think you could explain just by reading it. Always pray before Bible studies!

- John 4:22-24 - God is a Spirit
- John 3:5 - Water baptism is not enough
- Joel 2:28 - a prophecy 100's of years before Jesus about the Holy Ghost
- Acts 2:15-21- Peter ties their experience and tongue-talking to Joel's prophecy
- Isaiah 28:11 - What is the Holy Ghost? God

talking through people

- Isaiah 43:18-19 - God once talked through prophets, but will later do a “new thing”
- Isaiah 28:12 - The feeling of the Holy Ghost is refreshing
- ACTS 3:19-20 - The Holy Ghost is Jesus, come to be with you
- EZEKIEL 36:26-27 - Another prophecy, of the Holy Ghost, and it’s effects
- Matthew 3:11 - John tells of Jesus, and the Holy Ghost. Jesus came, why not the HG?
- John 14:26 - Holy Ghost comes, like baptism, in Jesus name. Not evil or weird
- Mark 16:17 - Not just a difference in your speech, but is a power in spirit
- Acts 2:1-4 - The first Holy Ghost experience, for 120 people
- Acts 2:38-39 - Peter says it’s for everyone
- Acts 10:44-47 - The Holy Ghost comes with speaking in tongues, that’s how Jews knew it was the same as theirs
- Acts 11:15-17 - How did he know it was the Holy Ghost? Tongue-talking, like at first
- Acts 19:2 & 6 - Holy Ghost comes through prayer

- 1 Corinthians 14:18 & 39 - Paul says he speaks in tongues a lot, and wouldn't stop it
- Romans 8:9 & 11 - Without the Holy Ghost inside, we are not with Christ and not saved

* Ask them "are you ready to receive that Holy Ghost promise?"

* Tell them about repentance, to repent totally (asking God's help to repent of everything) and then get them baptized. The Holy Ghost follows obedience, into empty, sinless people.

What a Christian should live like

There is already a Theme for this subject in the book "Hack Your Bible/ Mods" but if you want a good, step by step Bible study proving the need for a Holy Lifestyle, here you go. I understand if you don't feel qualified to just start pointing out scriptures.

* This is not an exhaustive study; there is much more *

Follow the directions in HYB/Mods chapter "The Built in 'Chain Bible Study." Here you're given a list of scriptures in a certain order to draw a square around and reference forward in progression. There is also a little note on this sheet what the verse is about, to copy next to the verse if you don't think you could explain just by reading it. Always pray before Bible studies!

- I Cor 6:19 - Are you His or not? Then act like it
- I Cor 7:22-23 - True freedom is the ability to do what is right, not to do whatever evil we can think of
- I Pet 1:15,16 - Holiness living is a matter of identifying with your God
- II Corinthians 5:20 "Now then we are ambassadors for Christ"

- Heb 12:14 - God demands holiness: complete or partial?
- I Thes 4:1-9 - Some specific commands with the principles mixed in
- I Thes 5:22-24 - There is supposed to be a change when we become Christian
- II Cor 6:14-17 - The must be purity all through you, not just your heart
- Rom 12:1-2 - This "living sacrifice" is a change of lifestyle
- Phil 2:12-14 - Consistency of faith because we are a light in the world
- Matthew 5:14 - Light of the world, again
- Proverbs 27:12 - We know where living un-holy leads, we need to be wise
- JEREMIAH 35:1-19 - The Rechabites lived by rules of sobriety, and were blessed
- Ephesians 2:8 - Holiness won't save you - it's a response to that grace
- James 2: 14 - Faith demands action
- I Cor 6:12 - Freedom shouldn't be abused
- I Samuel 16: 7 - The Lord looks at the heart also, not exclusively
- Mark 10:19 - Honesty

- I Tim 2:8-10 - Modesty in dress
- Deut 22:5 - Distinction of the sexes in dress
- I Cor 11:1-6 - Distinction of the sexes in hair length
- I Pet 3:1-5 - Rejection of adornment
- Jer 1:5 , Zech 12:1 , Mat 5:21 Sanctity of Human life (includes suicide and abortion)
- I Cor 6:9 Sexual purity demanded
- Rom 6: 17-20 - Choosing life or death through our actions
- Matt 7: 20 Our actions label us

:Systems:

How we interact with and think about the Bible is just as important as the tools we use, if not more important. All the tools in the world won't save you if you don't act on the Bible's actual plan of salvation.

This section is all about your mindset when studying...These are not to be skipped

In the other chapters we explore ways to change and improve the physical Bible. We also look at outside resources that can assist our Bible study success. But now we look at you. We look at how you can change your perspective just a little to become a better student of the Bible.

This book's subtitle could have been "executions," but an out of context reading of the title might have created alarm. Acting on, executing the Bible in life, is the subject here. I'm offering you systems to memorize and apply the Bible. I'm giving some of what what supports the Bible as a supernatural source of truth. I'm trying to bring the other books together in this one and into your heart.

What You Should Know: //About the Bible//

The Bible is an amazing book that can easily be called a miracle, found in every Walmart.

Following are some facts; not one book compares to the Bible and these are some proofs. Not one other manuscript or book has affected the world so much, and nothing like it could ever be replicated in the same way by humanity alone. The Bible is amazing!

Here are some facts about your Bible:

- What does "testament" mean?

Testament means "covenant," "contract," or "promise." In the Bible covenants are often made between God and people.

- Who wrote the Bible?

The Bible was written under the inspiration of the Holy Spirit by over 40 different authors from all walks of life: shepherds, farmers, tent-makers, physicians, fishermen, priests, philosophers and kings. Despite these differences in occupation and the massive span of years it took to write it, the Bible is an extremely cohesive book.

- Which single author contributed the most books to the Old Testament?

Moses. He wrote the first five books of the Bible, referred to as the Pentateuch.

- Which single author contributed the most books to the New Testament?

The Apostle Paul, who wrote 14 books (over half) of the New Testament.

- When was the Bible written?

It was written over a period of some 1,500 years, from around 1450 B.C. (the time of Moses) to about 100 A.D. (following the death and resurrection of Jesus Christ).

- What is the oldest book in the Old Testament?

Many scholars agree that Job is the oldest book in the Bible, written by an unknown Israelite about 1500 B.C. Others hold that the Pentateuch (the first five books of the Bible) are the oldest books in the Bible, written between 1446 and 1406 B.C.

- What is the newest book in the New Testament?

The Book of Revelation is the youngest book of the New Testament, written about 95 A.D.

- What languages was the Bible written in?

The Bible was written in three languages: Hebrew, Aramaic, and Koine Greek.

- Are there "missing books of the Bible?"

The Bible was not written at one time, or even by one people. It is a collection of books inspired by the same God talking about that God's relationship with humanity. Because these books are inspired they have many commonalities in theme and style, and never conflict with each other.

Other old books have been included in some translations of the Bible, often the Apocrypha in Catholic translations, but these were all known of and *rejected* by the scholars that compiled the early Bible. Other old and mystic writings are out-and-out fakes trying to create fame for the "discoverer." The reason neither of these groups are included in the Bible is because they do not agree with the miraculously cohesive scripture.

These books sometimes persist and are held up as being just as valuable as the Bible because they teach different things than the Bible, but can not stand on their own, or because they are "new" and they give the person presenting them a sort of status.

- When was the first translation of the Bible made into English?

1382 A.D., by John Wycliffe.

- When was the Bible printed?

The Bible was printed in 1454 A.D. by Johannes Gutenberg who invented the "type mold" for the printing press. It was the first book ever printed.

- Do the books of the Bible agree with each other all of the time?

Yes. All of the Bible agrees with all the rest of the Bible (if you are using a good Bible translation.)

Every trick tried to make the Bible appear that it conflicts with itself has been proven false and contrived. Over all this time, and with all these different authors and languages, the Bible agrees.

We can't even get educated politicians to agree on needed regulations today!

- What is the longest book in the Bible?

The book of Psalms.

- What is the shortest book in the Bible?

2 John.

- What is the longest chapter in the Bible?

Psalm 119

- What is the shortest chapter in the Bible?

Psalm 117

- What is the longest verse in the Bible?

Esther 8:9

- What is the shortest verse in the Bible?

John 11:35 “Jesus wept.” [28]

- Who was the oldest man that ever lived?

Methuselah who lived to be 969 years old (Genesis 5:27).

- Which book in the Bible does not mention the word "God?"

The book of Esther.

- Who were the two men in the Bible who never died but were caught up to heaven?

Enoch, who walked with God and was no more (Genesis 5:22-24).

Elijah, who was caught up by a whirlwind into heaven (II Kings 2:11).

- Who does the Bible say was the meekest man in the Bible (not including Jesus)?

Moses (Numbers 12:3).

- How many Biblical prophecies did Jesus fulfill?

Over 360[29]

---

[28] Unless you use the NIV in which Job 3:2 says "He said"

[29] I have a couple lists I’m verifying but some of them are including writings outside the Bible, which I’m not comfortable sharing. This would be an AWESOME theme to highlight in your Bible, though.

- Are the places in the Bible real?

Yes, in fact most of early archeology (think Indiana Jones) in the near east was based and founded successfully on the Bible.

- How much of science does the Bible agree with

There is no conflict between the Bible and the facts of science. There may be many conflicts between the Bible and the theories of scientists, and between the facts of science and the theories of so-called "Bible scholars."

- How many languages has the Bible been translated into?

The Holy Bible has been translated into 2,018 languages, with countless more partial translations, and audio translations (for unwritten languages).

(This is an enormous amount of translations. In comparison, Shakespeare, considered by many to be the master writer of the English language, has only been translated into 50 languages.)

- Is the Bible still the best-selling book in the world?

Yes!

//How do you think of your Bible?//

Changing how you think is an important hack. Genius has been said to only be a different view of the world. Great mechanics and artists don't see parts and strokes of a brush, they see systems and themes. We need to be open to the Bible as it was intended, and there are three major ways we can fail.

These are:

- Denying the authority of the Bible
- Reading into the Bible
- Only referencing the Bible, or using only parts

Denying the authority of the Bible is often labeled as a liberal tendency, but the most conservative circles are just as at risk of error. Liberals are condemned by their conservative counterparts for elevating reasoning and logic, the hallmark of Greece, to the same level as the Bible. The Bible talks about this in Col 2:8[30] They say "the Bible can't mean what it says, because it doesn't make sense to me." Then begins the tearing and twisting of scripture to include outside concepts, like and old-earth theory (evolution). They weaken the Bible by saying that logic and reason are just as important as the Bible in our understanding of God and His will.

Those labeled as conservatives can also deny the authority of the Bible by elevating tradition. "Traditionally we have always held this belief, or done this thing, or understood that this way" the liberals quote. This unbending stance is important when you are right, but how can we know we are right if we have not founded our stance in the Bible. The "traditions of men" are equally condemned in that same scripture, Col 2:8.

Hindus and Muslims have long traditions too, should we equally consider them? If tradition is raised up on the ladder of importance to be even with the Bible then we have failed to esteem God's word.

The second pitfall is Reading into the Bible. We do this when we look for scriptures that uphold our personal positions, instead of just reading the Bible.

---

30 "Beware lest any man spoil you through philosophy and vain deceit, after the tradition of men, after the rudiments of the world, and not after Christ." KJV

Who is the source of wisdom? And where is it found? If either of your answers involve "me" you are mistaken. To get all we can from the Bible we must leave everything else behind.

You will find this when speaking to trinitarians especially. They were raised, or have come to possess the idea, that there are three gods who are so similar that they are really the one God in the Bible.

They won't accept this paraphrase of their belief, insisting that the Godhead is too complex to concisely explain and that there is one God but also three gods at the same time, and "great is the mystery of godliness." They will read the thousands of references to God in the Bible where the context and describing words mean exclusively "one" and still see a trinity because they read into the Bible instead of from it.

Though you can twist scripture, that does not mean these are the intentions of the Bible. We must empty the vessel of our minds to capture what the Bible has for us, like a cup full of vinegar wanting to hold cream.

Only referencing the Bible is the last pitfall we'll discuss. It's often a symptom of reading into the Bible, but is a problem of it's own as well. If we only read what we've read, then how can we expect something new? It's scary to read the whole Bible, for some, because there's stuff in there that's hard to understand. There's old words and huge themes and a Hell too.

But "All scripture [is] given by inspiration of God" 2Ti 3:16[31]. If there are other verses that contradict what you believe, then your understanding is flawed. This method of using the whole Bible to find specific truth, and not just sound-bites, is called Systematic Theology. It's not the only way to study scripture, but it should be used by everyone.

So change the way you think. Ask yourself when you feel a conflict "am I going with the Bible on this one?" Look at the whole of scripture. Don't just accept what's easy if there's a conflict, sort it out and get more guidance. And as you search out the scriptures make sure you're really reading them. You could be reading into them.

---

[31] " All scripture [is] given by inspiration of God, and [is]... profitable for doctrine, for reproof, for correction, for instruction in righteousness:" KJV

//Memorizing the Books and Parts of the Bible in less than an hour//

If I could do it so can you.

I have failed history tests, and hated learning Spanish, because I am not naturally good at memorizing things. I'm a conceptual thinker; I like stories, plans, and formulas. I have never been good at memorizing facts or names. I'm the last person to ask a phone number from.

I later become a youth pastor. I was teaching and preaching, and I felt terrible. I didn't know the books of the Bible by heart. Wasn't there a song? Did I ever know them all? I'm not sure that I did. And that's bad for a minister. I felt bad about it, but what was I going to do?

I looked[32], and asked people, and found that

---

[32] This chapter is pretty much a paraphrase of this series: http://www.deliverfreedom.com/blog/how-to-memorize-the-books-of-the-bible-%E2%80%93-part-1-%E2%80%93-overall-structure/ they include audio recording walking you though the process- I certainly suggest you visit.

there was another way to memorize things. It's a combination of what is called the Associative Memory Technique and Loci Memory System. You essentially associate the parts of the Bible with parts of your body, and then create ridiculous images that are phonetically similar to the books of the bible on those parts.

If this sounds hard it's not, it's actually quite fun!

First Part: Building from the Body

On each of your body parts we are putting a section of the Bible. This is useful because the parts of the Bible hold different things, like histories and prophecies. Later, you won't have to sing a whole song to find what book that is, or where it is; you'll just think about what it's subject is and jump right to it.

Parts of your Body we will use: your toes, your knees, your thigh muscle, your rear, your lungs, your shoulders, your collar, your face, your forehead. Think of yourself sitting down. Now we'll add parts to each of these areas.

The Bible is divided up into two major divisions, the Old Testament and the New Testament. I think that everybody knows that so we do not need any kind of memory techniques to figure that out.

Most people however are not aware that there are nine major segments in the books of the Bible. I am going to show you how to first of all commit those nine major segments to your memory.

1. Toes - 5 books of Moses

Moses is your trigger here. And I think that most of you probably have a picture in your mind how Moses might look. Maybe an older gentleman with a long white or gray beard and long gray hair, maybe even carrying the Ten Commandments. He could be dropping the Ten Commandments on your toes. Glue Moses to your toes.

2. Knees - History, or the Story of the Nation of Israel

Imagine a nation of little people on your knees telling you a story. Imagine all the little people, what they'd wear and how they might sound - getting the image to stick is super important, so make it real.

3. Thigh Muscles - Wisdom Books

Personally, I use a brain to represent wisdom. You might use a wisdom tooth if you want, but I use the brain. I just want you to imagine a goopy brain right there on your thighs.

4. Rear - Major Prophets

There are five of them, but for right now, just remember "Major Prophets." Create a tripper for Major Prophets by imagining a Major like in the Army or in the Navy. Glue that image to your rear. That is "Major Prophets."

5. Lungs - Minor Prophets

In or on your lungs, I want you to imagine a coal miner. He is coughing and wearing a helmet with a light on it, and he is carrying a pick ax. That is a miner and it represents the Minor Prophets on your lungs.

So take a second to review those. On your lungs, you have a Minor Prophet, on your rear, you have the Major Prophet, on your muscle, you have the Wisdom books, on your knees and they are telling you that Story about the History of the Nation of Israel. Lastly, on your toes, who is dropping the tablets with the Ten Commandments? That it right, it is the five books of Moses. Very good!

6. Shoulders - Gospels, or Life of Jesus

Now the next major segment of the books of the Bible is the life of Jesus. Where is that going go? That is going to go on your shoulders. So most of you probably have a picture of what Jesus would look like to you, so just imagine him. He is riding up there on your shoulders to represent the life of Jesus and the early church.

7. Collar - Paul's Letters

"Paul" sounds like "Ball." On your collar, I want you to imagine a ball that has got letters of the alphabet all over it. That is that ball of letters triggering Paul's Letters. You're not losing the letters, they're all wrapped up and making a ball.

8. Face - Apostle's Letters

So how could you create a picture for Apostle's Letters? I would imagine an envelope that has postal stamps all over it. It is a postal letter. That image represents the Apostle's letters.

9. Point of forehead - Prophecy

On your forehead. I want you to just imagine a professor. Phonetically, Professor and Prophecy are pretty much exactly the same. So if you have done that vividly and utilizing some action the will be strongly glued to you body.

Let's review, going backwards from your forehead point:

Forehead Point – Professor for the Prophecy Section

Face – Postal letters representing the Apostle's Letters

Collar – Ball with letters for Paul's letters

Shoulders – Jesus for the life of Jesus and the early church

Lungs – Coal miner representing the Minor Prophets

Rear – Army Major for the Major Prophets

Thigh Muscle – Brain symbolizing the Wisdom Literature

Knees – They are telling you that story about the Nation of Israel

Toes – Moses for the five books of Moses.

Take a second and review all those. You might even want to jot them down.

Second Part - Old Testament

So we tied the parts of your body to parts of the Bible, now we are going to associate strange, weird pictures that will stick in your mind to the books of the Bible. They will sound like the books, kind of, at least enough to give you a hint and trigger the name of the book.

These crazy scenes are going to take place on the parts of your body that correlate to the correct parts of the Bible. It's important that these scenes are preposterous and vivid so that you remember them. Take the time to really imagine them, how they would look, sound, and smell.

1. Toes - 5 books of Moses

Your first body part you used is your toes, and right now Moses is standing there.

The five books of Moses are Genesis, Exodus, Leviticus, Numbers and Deuteronomy. How do you make that into a picture?

You have Moses on there already, but what is he doing? We are going to need to make a story out of this, so I want you to just imagine this as vividly as you can. You have Moses on your toes, now from his chin, which phonetically is exactly the same as Chin-e-sis or Genesis, from Moses's chin he has suspended and acts and ducts, or Ex-odus.

Moses pulls on a pair of Levi's jeans that are all covered with tics, that is Levi-tics, Leviticus. From the pockets of those Levi's jeans, he pulls out two birds, but they cannot feel anything, because they are numb-birds or Numbers.

He looks at you and yells at the top of his lungs, he says, "Dude! Run!" That is dude-run-omy.

Genesis – Chin(esis)

Exodus – Act and ducts

Leviticus – Levi jeans covered in tics

Numbers – Numb birds

Deuteronomy – Dude run!

Review this as many times as you need to get it to stick, but this wild picture should be remembered easily.

2. Knees - History, or the Story of the Nation of Israel

Next section, on your knees, what have you got? Your knees are telling you the story or the history of the nation of Israel. There are 12 books here. Watch this! They are Joshua, Judges, Ruth, 1 and 2 Samuel, 1 and 2 Kings, 1 and 2 Chronicles, Ezra, Nehemiah and Ester. How do you make that picture?

Your knees are telling you the story, which is sound based, but I want you to envision the story unfolding on your knees. From your knees, I want you to imagine sprouting a huge Joshua tree.

There is a Joshua tree sprouting out of your knees and here is what you see in the branches of that tree. On the far left hand side, you see a bunch of Judges engaged in a very animated conversation with Babe Ruth, the big baseball player from the early 1900s.

Next to the Judges that are talking with Babe Ruth, you see standing next to each other are two mules that are covered with sand, they are sand-mules, or "Samuel"s. Riding on each of the mules is a king, so you have two Kings. Picture them with their big crowns and their long flowing robes. Now each of these kings is holding in his hand a chrome nickel for Chronicle.

Next to that scene with the mules and the kings and the chrome nickel, you see a zebra which would be a representation for Ezra. The zebra is using his knee, for Nehemiah, to stir the dirt the shape of an "S" for Ester.

Joshua – Joshua tree

Judges – Judges

Ruth – Babe Ruth

Samuel – Sand mules

Kings – Kings

Chronicles – Chrome nickels

Ezra – Zebra

Nehemiah – Knee

Ester – Stir S.

3. Thigh Muscles - Wisdom Books

The Wisdom books there are only five books, Job, Psalm, Proverbs, Ecclesiastes and the Song of Solomon.

This group of books is symbolized by a brain, but what is that brain doing on your muscle? The brain pulls on a robe that symbolizes Job. This robe is made of palm leaves and very soft fur on the inside, Palms and Prov-furs . The brain is eating a chocolate eclair and drinking tea at the same time. An eclair and tea for Ecclesiastes. While the brain is eating, it is singing songs.

So that brain is pulling on a rope that is made of palm with fur on the inside eating an eclair and drinking tea and singing songs. That is Job, Psalm, Proverbs, Ecclesiastes and Song of Solomon. Boom! That all lives right there on your muscle.

Job – Robe

Psalm – Palm leaves

Proverbs – (pro)Fur

Ecclesiastes – ecclair and tea

Song of Solomon – Songs

[see image for my mind's eye]

4. Rear - Major Prophets

The next file on your body is your rear. You have a military major there, not a general, but a major to symbolize the Major Prophets. Picture him wearing a full uniform. What is he doing? He looks at you right in the eye and he says, "I say!" to symbolize Isaiah. He then jumps up on a chair that looks at him with one gigantic sad eye in the seat, which is a chair-eye or a Chair-emiah! Now the next book is Lamentations, so this major looks down and notices that he is standing on a whole bunch of mints, for Lamentations. Then he realizes they would be very easy to kill. He would be an Easy Kill or Ezekiel, he jumps of that chair and he yells, "Dang!" That's his dang-yell, or Daniel.

Isaiah – "I say!"

Jeremiah – Chair eye

Lamentations – Mints

Ezekiel – Easy kill

Daniel – "Dang!"

5. Lungs - Minor Prophets

The Minor Prophets are next, now this is a tough one because there are 12 of them. Hosea, Joel, Amos, Obadiah, Jonah, Micah, Nahum, Habakkuk, Zephaniah, Haggai, Zechariah and Malachi. This is how you make a picture out of them:

Right now you have a coal miner on your lungs wearing a hat with a light, holding a pick ax, for the minor prophets. Now this miner grabs a hose, like a big fire hose, for Hosea, and starts spraying GI Joe, for Joel.

When he hits GI Joe with that fire hose, a mosquito, for Amos(quito), comes flying off the of them and starts flapping his wings in the air. Now this mosquito magically transforms himself into a bat. It's not just any bat, it is an old bat, with one hanging old eye. Old-Bat-Eye for Obadiah. Yeah it's weird, but you'll be able to remember it!

As this mosquito is turned into an old bat eye, the whole scene is swallowed up by a giant whale. What would the whale represent? Of course, I think everybody knows the story of Jonah and the whale.

The whale is holding a microphone, but he is holding the microphone to his knee. Yes, in this story whales have knees; just create the picture in your mind. The microphone obviously is for Micah.

The whale is holding the microphone to his knee because his knee is making the strange humming sound. It is a knee-hum or Nahum. On the back of the whale you are seeing in your mind's eye, I want you to picture a cook. A cook with white clothes on, a big white hat on and he is real happy, so he has a big smile on his face. He's a happy cook, for Habakkuk.

The happy cook is holding a few things. In one hand a fan with a great big eye on it. That is a Ze-fan-iah. And the other hand, he is holding a grocery bag with that same looking eye on it. That is the bag-eyes, sounds just like Haggai. Again, all we are looking to do is create triggers. He pours out the bag and what comes tumbling out is a zucchini that is crying. A zucchini crying for Zechariah, and a melon that is crying, for Malachi. Done!

Hosea – Hose

Joel – GI Joe

Amos – A mosquito

Obadiah – Old bat eye

Jonah – Whale

Micah – Microphone

Nahum – Knee hum

Habakkuk – Happy cook

Zephaniah – Fan eye

Haggai – Bag eyes

Zechariah – Zucchini crying

Malachi – Melon crying

Now you have it. Go back and review these things. It might take you a couple of times through, so take it one file at a time. When you have one, move on to the next one. I promise it won't take very long at all.

Third Part - New Testament

6. Shoulders - Gospels, or Life of Jesus

The next section is our shoulders. So now on our shoulders, who have you got riding up there? That is right; you have got Jesus sitting on your shoulders. Now there are five books in the next section here, which is the life of Jesus in the early church. The five books, most of you know the four Gospels, Matthew, Mark, Luke and John and then there is one other book that tells the whole story of the life of the early Christian church. That is the book of Acts.

Matthew – Mat (like a doormat)

Mark – (Magic) marker

Luke – Loop (of rope)

John – Toilet (no offense to anybody, but that is already a picture)

Acts – Ax

If you have made that picture with action and emotion, and have done it clearly in your mind, you now have the first five books of the New Testament filed to your shoulders which is Matthew, Mark, Luke, John and Acts. Bingo!

7. Collar - Paul's Letters

Next, the letters from the Apostle Paul. What do

we have on your collar right now? It is a ball with letters all over it. Now, we need to create some action that is going to get us Romans, 1 and 2, Corinthians, Galatians, Ephesians, Philippians, Colossians 1 and 2, Thessalonians, 1 and 2 Timothy, Titus and Philemon.

Now again, you may already have these pictures created into a story that the ball is acting out on your collar, but if you do not, here is how I would do it. I want you to imagine that ball puts on a big Roman helmet and then shoves two apple cores into his mouth. You have to imagine it like a cartoon.

That ball then puts on a pair of galoshes, walks up to an elephant, picks up a Phillips head screwdriver and starts scraping coal off of the elephant's shins. He then puts down the Phillips head screwdriver, grabs two thistles which are real sharp and they have got spines sticking out of them. Off of these two thistles, are two moths, who are wearing ties. But they are not wearing these ties on their neck, they are wearing them on their toes. Once those moths fly off with ties around their toes, the ball picks up a lemon and starts filing the skin off of that lemon.

The books here have been left out of this series of images. You should stop and make the connections yourself. The reason is: this is a great system to remember anything! You can make up pictures for anything you want to remember, and put them in any place. You have many buildings and parks that you know full of places to put scenes and pictures like we have just now on your body.

Romans – Roman helmet

Corinthians – Two apple core (inthians)

Galatians – Galoshes

Ephesians – Elephant

Philippians – Phillips head screwdriver

Colossians – Scraped the coal off of his shins

Thessalonians – Thistle spines

Timothy – Two (Tim) moths that flew off

Titus – Ties on their toes

Philemon. – File a Lemon

8. Face - Apostle's Letters

We are almost done here, you guys. You are doing great. We only have two more segments to go and they are smaller ones.

On your face, you have a postal letter for the Apostle's Letters. Here are they again, what are the books? They are Hebrews, James 1 and 2, Peter, 1, 2 and 3 John then Jude. Here is a real easy way to do this.

Hebrews you can make a brew into a broom. That postal letter has a broom in its hands. Again, you have got to imagine like a cartoon. This broom has chains wrapped around it. He is using this broom and he sweeps two egg beaters and they go right underneath three toilets that you see lined up. Picture it clearly. Now inside of those toilets, all of three of them are filled up with jewels.

So the brooms with the chains, sweep the two egg beaters under three toilets. You have to see each one of them. The 3 Johns that are filled up and overflowing with jewels or Jude. Bingo! That is on your face. You remember...

Hebrews – Broom

James – Chains

Peter – Egg beaters

John – Toilet

Jude – Jewel

9. Point of forehead - Prophecy

Now the last one, which is on your forehead point, and has a professor on it because it is the Prophecy section. There is only one book in it, the book of Revelation. I would picture that professor giving a lecture about a revolution. Or he could be giving a lecture on two "rival nations."

Either way, if you picture that professor giving this lecture and spinning this story about some sort of war that is the revolution or it is between two rival nations, either one would get you the picture for Revelations on the point of your head.

Revelations – Revolution or two rival nations.

Done!

So there you have it. Just like that. It probably took you about 30 to 45 minutes of actual study time total.

You now have all 66 books of the Bible committed to memory!

If you want to lock them in long term, go back to the list numerous times, giving yourself spaced repetition – one hour, one day, and one week. Review this material in the next hour, review it again in the next 24 hours and come back to it in a few days. You will be amazed how well that information will stick with you.

//Prayer//

You may think this "prayer" section is obligatory. You might think I "have to" write about this, but I don't. It's my guide; I'll write what I like. And I like prayer. I enjoy talking to God. When trying to apply your Bible, no single element will be as powerful as prayer.

The Bible says that the "the Spirit of truth, is come, he will guide you into all truth" Jhn 16:13. The most often undervalued part of Bible study is prayer. Yet prayer is essential to gaining wisdom and understanding when you read God's Word. Through prayer, you can approach God and acknowledge your incomplete knowledge of his Word, as well as your need for Him to open your heart to his wisdom. So decide to begin each time of study with prayer.

Prayer isn't just useful before reading, though; we should pray about what we read afterward. Some would call this "meditating" on the Bible. Once His word is in your mind you still need help to apply to your heart, and to remember it in times of need. It also helps you to examine your life in light of what God reveals in his Word.

You should add to your post reading prayer a list of personal questions, which might lead you to pray a little more specifically.

- Is there any sin mentioned in the passage that I need to confess of and stop doing?
- Is there a command given that I should obey?
- Is there a promise made that I can apply to my life, or that supports me right now?
- Is there a example given that I could follow?

If the answer to any of these is “yes” then you have found a specific prayer to pray, after your reading. Like was said at the beginning of this guide; pray more.

A Prayer Hack: the Ladder

... For the inside of your Bible's cover

Draw a ladder with twelve steps, large enough to write a phrase above each. The phrases are going to be types of prayers for you to do when praying for an extended amount of time. A depiction on the next page is typed out. Use it from the bottom to top, ascending closer to God through prayer.

Pray for 5 minutes on each and you will have prayed for an hour straight! For 1/2 hour of prayer pray on only 6 steps; for 2 hours pray a full 10min on each step. It's a great system that's been advocated by many to get used to praying for extended periods of time.

This is not the only way to pray, but during prayer meeting now you can fill the time instead of just fighting sleep. Mix it in, and see what happens. Teach some younger people to use it. Now you don't need inspiration to settle down and talk to God; just open up your Bible.

Steps 1 through 12, 5min each

Bottom to top

|_______________________| *(Done!)*

| Praise! _______________ | *Acknowledge His Greatness*

| Use Songs/Psalms ____ | *Pray a song or Psalm*

| Intercede ____________ | *Pray for other's needs*

| Wait on God__________ | *Hard, but biblical*

| Ask Direction _________ | *"God, what should I do?"*

| Visit His Promises_____ | *What has God Promised ?*

| Meditate _____________ | *Think on what you read*

| Read the Word ______ | *Open your Bible and read*

| Share Your Needs ____ | *Tell Him what you need*

| Testify of His Goodness | *Remind yourself of it all*

| Repentance __________ | *Get clean of the past*

| Praise God __________ | *Celebrate His Greatness*

| | *(^Start)*

//How to: Read your Bible EVERYday//

We've heard it from pastors for years, "You (heathens) need God's word EVERYday!" And we shout "AMEN!" There's no denying that God's word would improve every day- every time we try it we're blessed. Even just thinking about it, it makes sense. No argument here, pastor!

Except in our actions.

We fight it a lot with our actions; we surf the 'net and shower extra long and forget the word of God in our daily grind.

Forget the word of God? Wasn't it that same "word" that created all this? Wouldn't it be foolish to ignore the power that would come from enjoying that word daily? Yup. I'm not making excuses for you but I am saying I understand. The grind gets us.

For a very long time, even into the time I decided ministering, daily Bible reading was a struggle. In my head I was all about it- but in practice I hadn't read my Bible every day for a week, ever. No excuses given. I was failing to make God's word an important part of my life.

So, much like the Memorizing the books of the Bible part of this guide, shame drove me to find an answer. I knew there were benefits; mountains of benefits waited on little ol' Seagraves. He could be

> The Proverbs trick
>
> Did you know there are 31 chapters in Proverbs? That's just about one for every day of the month. Did you know that Proverbs is combined with nearly all new testament-only copies of the Bible? Did you know that Proverbs was written by the wisest man in the Bible?
>
> One way to get your Bible reading for the day is to simply read the chapter of Proverbs that correlates to the day of the month. Sure chapter 31 might get skipped every other month, but your Bible reading won't!

transformed into seeing the world as God does, filled with love and power, free from worries and doubts. He could stand on a mountain of Biblical testimony. Seagraves could climb out of his bad habits by establishing this one good one. If only he could start up the path.

After experimentation and many hours of study, here is what I know: You can make the Bible a part of every day. You should, sure, but we "should workout" too. Here's the message, you CAN; and here's my system.

How to make Bible reading an EVERYday thing

1. Make Bible reading a part of your identity

"I'm not that guy" is a phrase that has served me extremely well.

When other folks told me I should back out and give up saying "I'm not that guy" would save me. When I wanted to go into debt, but knew I was crippling my future if I did, I said "I'm not that guy."

Not being "that guy" was a decision I made because there were other things more important. It's not that I'm so strong, I'm just not the guy that backs down or sets myself up for failure. It's my identity.

I am the guy that does what it takes to make things happen, who will sacrifice what others won't to get what others can't. I am the guy that escalates the situation to win. I am a reader, and strategist, and a supporter of others. I am the guy who cheers for his friends. I want to be excellent in ministry, and aware in the Spirit enough to act on what God wants. And I want to be a Bible reader, every day. So I decided to be.

In the end it's all about who you decide to be.

Joshua made a decision: as for me and my house? we will serve the Lord. "I'm that guy" he said.

You need to frame what you want to do (or even want to be free from doing) within the context of a moral quest. You need to see how this, Bible reading specifically, is a part of the big picture of who you are. Every time you read your Bible you are personally defining who you are. God said "I am that I am," I believe this is true for each of us; we are simply who we are, and who we are is up to us.

I'm a Bible reading, real Christian, who is connected to God through prayer and His word. So of course I read the Bible every day. That's how this first step works.

2. Make it routine - pair it

This is simple. The best time to read your Bible is in the morning. Two reasons: it's a great start to your day, knowing that there is a God and that He cares for you enough to preserve inspired texts for thousands of years so you can read them. And second, because it will influence the rest of your day. From that reminder of God on, you are primed to be a man or woman of God.

> You might check out the "Lift" app if you have a smart phone. It's how I've been creating good habits, and tracking my Bible reading.

So, look at your morning routine, and pair your Bible

reading with something you already do every morning. For me? It's a morning cup of coffee. I love coffee, and whenever I drink it alone I include the Bible. Simple! I always drink coffee in the morning, during and after breakfast, so I always have a trigger to remember my Bible reading.

For my professionals out there: check out www.BiblePlan.org . They will email you your daily reading, and you know you're already checking your inbox "religiously." There's a couple of good plan options including chronological. For me? This was a killer option working in an office in the oilfield.

Other morning routines to pair with might be: post exercise, while riding the bus to work, at breakfast, as quiet time before the office opens up, or to wind down after the kids go to bed. I'm not judging here. Just get it done.

3. Pray

This is covered in more detail later, but prayer will get you more out of your reading. And if you're receiving great benefits it will be easier to continue the habit. Pray before and after reading.

4. Use a trial period

This is common in habit creation exercises. Take two weeks and make this a super focus, like it's written on your doors and coffee maker “read Bible.” After two weeks you can take those down, trial’s over. But hopefully you have started a habit that will stick.

You might also use trial periods for different routines. So maybe you’ll try making quiet time before work to read, for two weeks, and if that isn’t working you try another routine. Eventually you find one that does work. Taking trial periods will get you there by giving you enough time to identify what isn’t working and what might be better.

5. Make the Bible accessible

Simple, but if your Bible is nowhere near your coffee you might get distracted and play a game on your phone instead. Or you might forget your Bible for your bus ride. I would suggest keeping your Bible in the same spot always, and having a copy in the same translation on your phone. Then it’s always where you can find it (building a stronger routine) and it’s always accessible if your forget it.

6. Have a plan

Many people don’t know where to start reading. That’s fair; it’s a huge book. Look at Bible reading plans. I’ve included some in the Apps section of this book. Having a plan gets you right into the word of God- not confusion or wasted time!

7. Have a favorite part of the Bible

This is especially good if you forget your regular Bible with it's plan. In this case you can use any Bible and still read. Places to find Bibles are: on your phone, online at BLB.org with any computer, in any library or book store, or in a hotel room.

If you have a favorite part of the Bible you're always ready to read. Many people really enjoy the Gospels (Mt. Mk. Lk. Jn.) because they tell about the life of Jesus. The Wisdom Books in the Old Testament have been a constant favorite for me, since I'm young and need wisdom. Of these I'm in constantly in Proverbs and Ecclesiastes. Now days I've been reading a lot of the Prophets, seeing their lifestyle and commitment to proclaiming God's will for the people. Psalms is also a very popular "go to" book of the Bible for it's beauty and uplifting themes.

Now if you're missing your plan you can still start reading your Bible right away.

You can read. You have a Bible.

Every day you can read that Bible.

What was holding you back before was motivation and possibly that you didn't have a system. I hope we've fixed that here. If there's something you'd like to add, maybe a tip or encouragement to others, feel free to Tweet[33] us or post on our Facebook[34]:

33 http://www.twitter.com/PDerrickS

34 http://www.facebook.com/HackYourBible

//Using BLB.org//

BLB.org is one of my favorite resources, and deserves this space in our Hacker guide. Later other resources might be sent to the supporters of HYB+ through email, but this is the top of the list. Evangelical in it's roots (so Calvinist/ reformed) the commentaries and resource books they offer fall under the warning of the Commentaries in this guide- but if you can eat the meat and not choke on the bones, you'll be blessed by this tool.

From the website:

"Web-based technology is our platform, and we've been working at it since the mid 1990's at a time when personal computers were only beginning to surface in mainstream public. Little did we know then that the years and years of programming every little detail of various Bible translations, original languages, commentaries, and study aids would eventually be available on millions of personal computers, cell phones, and tablets! ... We are living in exciting days where millions of people around the world have an opportunity to read and study God's Word through web-based technology. Many more will have access in the years ahead. And for those who do not have access due to difficult living situations or persecution, we are continuing to work on ways of getting our comprehensive Bible study tool into their hands as well."

I use BLB.org mostly for it's built in Strong's concordance (with numbers and quick links to all other uses, and that will even pronounce the Greek words for you! BLB.org also has a great linking system to scripture, compares Bible translations one right after another, and helps in finding that partially quoted verse in the back of my mind. If you're musically gifted, they also link what hymns use the scripture as well. Once you've looked up a scripture, hover over the blue buttons to the left of it to see what they offer.

There are many maps, a great time-line, and other helps that make this free resource more valuable than many paid applications.

When I'm working on sermons it's a huge help to see what the original language was, how it was used throughout the Bible, and how others have interpreted the passage. I love to see the hymns that were written from the Bible. Often some context builder is also tied in.

* A portion of the proceeds of from the sale of HYB+ will be donated to BLB.org to keep this great resource online.

:Repairs:

//Binding Repair//

The simple rule, if this is a good Bible that you want to keep for a long time, is retire the Bible. Lay it flat on a shelf, maybe in a cover that doesn't bend of stress the cover, and leave it be used in the future sparingly. You likely value this Bible for it's notes and history, and these can be kept forever as long as you don't take it out and about and start losing pages. Now go buy a good Bible that will outlast that one.

You can have a bible rebound, if the binding is the problem, for about the cost of a good new Bible. It's up to you whether to follow this route. A company that has been suggested to me, with very high reviews, is Leonard's Books, found online.[35] By all accounts their bindings and covers last lifetimes! I considered hacking a Thompson Chain Bible, and

---

[35] http://www.leonardsbooks.com/

then getting them to rebind it with all the resources in HYB+.

//Repairing Tears in Pages//

For tears in the paper or dust jacket, use Gaylord or any document repair tape.[36] This is a tissue tape that is peeled from the backing and applied. The instructions are on the box. Wash hands before using and apply very carefully. It only gives you one chance.

NEVER use cellophane tape. It's very acidic and will turn brown and drop off over time, leaving an ugly stain on your paper.

//Hinge & Cover Repair//

For hinge repair, use Eco-Flo Leather Weld. This is a water-based laminate that is designed for leather to paper, but actually works better from paper to

---

[36] http://www.gaylord.com/adblock.asp?abid=15555

paper and paper to fabric. It is the same pH-balanced adhesive that is sold as "archival glue" by conservation binders, but is sold by Leather Factory[37] for about half the price. It is non-toxic, water reversible, and permanently elastic.

Your cover can't truly be repaired on the outside, usually. Your best course of action is to use the same document repair tape on the inside/ back of the cover so that it's not seen. This tape is still flexible and won't damage the cover.

A further option you might try, at some risk, is to contact an interior repair specialist through a car lot. These skilled craftsmen (who you should ask for an example of their work) can sometimes build up, glue, and dye leather to look new. Their profession is to do this to car interiors.

The very best option is of course to replace the cover with a professional.

---

[37] http://www.tandyleatherfactory.com/en-usd/home/department/liquids-n/liquids-n.aspx

//Simple leather Restoration and Care//

Care

- Store leather-bound books in the shade. Don't let direct sunlight shine on them. The UV light deteriorates the leather. This means you should not be leaving your Bible on the dashboard, no matter how convenient.
- Also store them flat or on their spine, as with time any over-hang of the cover will crush.
- Remove from humid places, like basements and bathrooms. Molding is a problem.
- Apply an oil-free leather conditioner, such as Lexol, to the cover of the book, following the instructions on the packaging. Do this about twice a year.

Cleaning

- When it needs cleaning, rub a large soft eraser over the cover.
- Apply a mixture of ammonia and water to a non-dyed, cotton cloth. Only apply enough to barely wet the cloth. Rub the cloth over the cover of the book to remove mildew.

//Mold Fighting//

Mold in pages is an ugly problem that will actually deteriorate your Bible quickly. Something to note; many people have mold allergies. There is no reason to assume you are immune. You should wear a dust mask at least while working with a moldy book.

To remove mold do the following:

Step 1:

Never introduce your Bible to a place that is damp or overly humid. Then is will not become moldy.

Done!

Step 2:

If this can not be helped, in the case of a flood or accident, or there is already mold in your Bible the next step is this. Put your Bible in a large zip-lock bag and freeze it for 24 hrs. This kills the mold and the spores. Then follow the next step.

Step 3:

Remove the Bible from the freezer and bag, put on some protection from the mold (like a mask), and use a dry sponge or toothbrush to dust off the mold from every page.

:Conclusion:

"Hack Your Bible" was a shock-title, I must admit. It was designed to get attention. I can't say that I'm sorry; I believe the Bible deserves more attention than we give it. In our daily lives many Christians never think of the Bible, even though it's quoted around us constantly. I hope to make you more aware.

This revolution you've started, by reading this book, is growing. Everyone I'm talking to about this subject is super pumped and getting involved. I'm getting suggestions left and right for more tips to include in a revision, already! If you enjoyed HYB+, or think it could benefit someone else, please do us the favor of Tweeting or posting on FB about the project. On Facebook there's a community of Bible hackers ready to boost you up and share even more tricks and tips!

In my dreams I see a generation of young people armed with Bible's they know inside and out. Their

Bibles are worn and thumbed through, and modified because they love them like they love their backpacks and sneakers. They want to get the truth OUT, and they're ready for whatever comes. This generation is happening now, and you spreading the word about resources like HYB+ and others is what's making it happen.

Some leaders are already starting groups to hack their Bibles together. I expect that they will have a stronger, more doctrinally sound group for their effort. Others are buying and using these guides as they buy new Bibles.

You could use this book as a way to break in a Bible, or to gift in addition to a Bible- I just want t=our movement to be more Bible literate. It's our foundation. If we leave the footing we climbed here on, we are trusting the mist of the clouds with our future. To many other movements have gone that way.

I don't expect that you would use every hack. I do expect to make some people more aware of what is available to them.

Hack Your Bible_Workshops

Derrick is available to lead 1 and 3 day workshops on this book's subject. These will leave your congregation with a passion to know their Bible better, and to want to share what they've learned with others. We expect a renewed focus on Bible studies and personal outreach after every meeting.

Additionally, every person in attendance receives FREE, full copies of the HYB ebooks so that they can continue their study of God's word. This isn't only an event, it is the start of a revival in leaning on and growing in God's Word.

Contact the author at www.PDerrickS.com

The Apostolic Pentecostal writing Movement

There is a weakness in the movement; we are not publishing enough. Many ministers and saints are tired of having to suggest outside books and then qualify them with warnings against false doctrine. The confusion these titles can cause has uprooted many souls in our past. We need to beat this. We can.

At the very same time there is a flood of content, wonderful testimonies and biblical insights, that has been waiting for someone to step up and publish. What has stalled these works in the past is the large investment needed for self publishing, or the loss of an author's rights to the book in traditional publishing companies.

Kingdom Publisher is the producer of this book you hold, and they are the premier publishing company for only Apostolic Pentecostal authors. Our team supports our authors with free resources, a super transparent process, and better compensation than traditional publishing ever has. We won't let the movement remain voiceless.

As a lean and fresh company authors are being published fast and inexpensively while they keep the rights to their books. Please go to our website:

www.KingdomPublisher.com

to learn how we can publish the author in your life.

If you're part of the movement and not one of our authors, we still want to hear from you and promote your book!

:End Resources:

All of these are available to you in email and printable format, if you go to page 85 and fill out a short form. If there are more freebies, or new items, we'll update you then! Thank you for purchasing this guide and we hope it's a real blessing!

For Theming: **O**neness, **H**oly Ghost, and **B**aptism verses

Gen

O 1:1

Ex

O 3:14

O 6:2-3

Deu

O 4:35

O 4:39

O 6:4

O 32:39

2 Sam

O 7:22

1 Kings

O 8:60

Job

O 13:8

Psalms

O 86:10

O 86:18

Isa

O 9:6

O 12:2

H 28:11-12

O 36:16

O 43:10-11

H 44:3

O 44:6, 24

O 45:5-6,14, 21-22

Jer

O 23:23-24

H 31:33

Joel

H 2:28-29

Zec

B 14:9

Mal

O 2:10

New Testament

Mat

O 1:18, 20, 23

B 1:21

H 3:11

B+O 28:19

Mark

O 12:29

B 16:16

H 16:17

Luke

O 1:35

H 3:16

H 11:13

B 24:47

H 24:49

John

O 1:1,14,33-34

B+H 3:3,5

O 3:34

H 4:14

O 4:24

O 5:22

O+B 5:43

H 7:38-39

O 8:24,58

O 10:30,33

O 14:6-11,16-18

O+B 14:26

H 16:13

O+B 17:6

O 20:28

Acts

H 1:4-5,8

H 2:1-11

H+B 2:37-39

H 2:41

H 3:19

B+O 4:12

H 4:31

H 5:32

O 7:59

H+B 8:12-17

B 8:36-39

O 9:5

H 9:17

B 9:18

H+B 10:44-48

H 11:13-17

B 16:31-33

O 17:27

H+B 19:2-6

O 20:28

B 22:16

Rom

B 6:3-4

H 8:1-17,26

O+B 10:12-13

B 6:11

1 Cor

B 1:13-16

H 3:16

O+B+H 6:9

B 6:11

O 8:4-6

H 12:3,13

H 13:1

H 14:2,4-5,14-15,18-19,22

2 Cor

O 4:4

O 5:19

H 13:14

Gal

H 3:14

B 3:27

H 4:6

H 5:22-23

Eph

O 1:11

H 1:13-14

O 3:9

O+B 4:4-6

Phil

O+B 2:9-11

Col

O 1:15-16,19

H 1:27

O 2:8-10

B 2:11-13

B 3:17

2 Thes

H 2:13

1 Tim

O 2:5

O 3:16

Titus

O 2:10,13

O 3:3-4

O+H+B 3:5-6

Heb

O 1:3-4

O 1:8

O 11:3

Jam

B 2:7

O 2:19

1 Pet

B 3:20-21	O 5:20	O 1:25
1 John	2 John	Rev
O 2:23	O 1:9	O 1:8
O 3:16	Jude	O 4:2

For Theming: 50 Prophecies Jesus Christ Fulfilled

Prophecies About Jesus - Old Testament References

Fulfillment - New Testament References

1. Messiah would be born of a woman.
   a. Genesis 3:15 Matthew 1:20 Galatians 4:4
2. Messiah would be born in Bethlehem.
   a. Micah 5:2 Matthew 2:1 Luke 2:4-6
3. Messiah would be born of a virgin.
   a. Isaiah 7:14 Matthew 1:22-23 Luke 1:26-31
4. Messiah would come from the line of Abraham.
   a. Genesis 12:3 Genesis 22:18 Matthew 1:1 Romans 9:5
5. Messiah would be a descendant of Isaac.
   a. Genesis 17:19 Genesis 21:12 Luke 3:34

6. Messiah would be a descendant of Jacob.
   a. Numbers 24:17 Matthew 1:2
7. Messiah would come from the tribe of Judah.
   a. Genesis 49:10 Luke 3:33 Hebrews 7:14
8. Messiah would be heir to King David's throne.
   a. 2 Samuel 7:12-13 Isaiah 9:7
   b. Luke 1:32-33 Romans 1:3
9. Messiah's throne will be anointed and eternal.
   a. Psalm 45:6-7 Daniel 2:44
   b. Luke 1:33 Hebrews 1:8-12
10. Messiah would be called Emmanuel.
    a. Isaiah 7:14 Matthew 1:23
11. Messiah would spend a season in Egypt.
    a. Hosea 11:1 Matthew 2:14-15
12. A massacre of children would happen at Messiah's birth place.
    a. Jeremiah 31:15 Matthew 2:16-18
13. A messenger would prepare the way for

Messiah

a. Isaiah 40:3-5 Luke 3:3-6

14. Messiah would be rejected by his own people.

    a. Psalm 69:8 Isaiah 53:3 John 1:11 John 7:5

15. Messiah would be a prophet.

    a. Deu. 18:15 Acts 3:20-22

16. Messiah would be preceded by Elijah.

    a. Malachi 4:5-6 Matthew 11:13-14

17. Messiah would be preceded by a forerunner

    a. Malachi 3:1 Luke 7:24.27

18. Messiah would be declared the Son of God.

    a. Psalm 2:7 Matthew 3:16-17

19. Messiah would be called a Nazarene.

    a. Isaiah 11:1 Matthew 2:23

20. Messiah would bring light to Galilee.

    a. Isaiah 9:1-2 Matthew 4:13-16

21. Messiah would speak in parables.

    a. Psalm 78:2-4 Isaiah 6:9-10
    b. Matthew 13:10-15, 34-35

22. Temple would become a house of merchandise

   a. Isaiah 56:7 Jeremiah 7:11 Matthew 21:13

23. Messiah would be sent to heal the brokenhearted.
    a. Isaiah 61:1-2 Luke 4:18-19
24. Messiah will heal blind, deaf, and lame
    a. Isaiah 35:5-6 Matthew 11:3-5
25. Messiah would be a priest after the order of Melchizedek.
    a. Psalm 110:4 Hebrews 5:5-6
26. Messiah would be called King.
    a. Psalm 2:6 Zechariah 9:9 Matthew 27:37 Mark 11:7-11
27. Messiah would be praised by little children.
    a. Psalm 8:2 Matthew 21:16
28. Messiah would be betrayed.
    a. Psalm 41:9 Zec. 11:12-13
    b. Luke 22:47-48 Matthew 26:14-16
29. Messiah's price money would be used to buy a potter's field.

a. Zec. 11:12-13 Matthew 27:9-10

30. Messiah would be falsely accused.

    a. Psalm 35:11 Mark 14:57-58

31. Messiah would be silent before his accusers.

    a. Isaiah 53:7 Mark 15:4-5

32. Messiah would be spat upon and struck.

    a. Isaiah 50:6 Matthew 26:67

33. Messiah would be hated without cause.

    a. Psalm 35:19 Psalm 69:4 John 15:24-25

34. Messiah would be crucified with criminals.

    a. Isaiah 53:12 Matthew 27:38 Mark 15:27-28

35. Messiah would be given vinegar to drink.

    a. Psalm 69:21 Matthew 27:34 John 19:28-30

36. Messiah's hands and feet would be pierced.

    a. Psalm 22:16 Zechariah12:10 John 20:25-27

37. Messiah would be mocked and ridiculed.

    a. Psalm 22:7-8 Luke 23:35

38. Soldiers would gamble for Messiah's garments.

    a. Psalm 22:18 Luke23:34

Matthew 27:35-36

39. Messiah's bones would not be broken.

    a. Exodus 12:46 Psalm 34:20 John 19:33-36

40. Messiah would be forsaken by God.

    a. Psalm 22:1 Matthew 27:46

41. Messiah would pray for his enemies.

    a. Psalm 109:4 Luke 23:34

42. Soldiers would pierce Messiah's side.

    a. Zechariah 12:10 John 19:34

43. Messiah would be buried with the rich.

    a. Isaiah 53:9 Matthew 27:57-60

44. Messiah would resurrect from the dead.

    a. Psalm 16:10 Psalm 49:15 Matthew 28:2-7 Acts 2:22-32

45. Messiah would ascend to heaven.

    a. Psalm 24:7-10 Mark 16:19 Luke 24:51

46. Messiah would be seated at God's right hand.

    a. Psalm 68:18 Psalm 110:1
    b. Mark 16:19 Matthew 22:44

47. Messiah would be a sacrifice for sin.

    a. Isaiah 53:5-12 Romans 5:6-8

48. Gentiles would seek Messiah
    a. Isaiah 9:2 Matthew 4:6
49. Messiah would send His Holy Spirit
    a. Joel 2:28 John 15:26
       Acts 2:16-17
50. Messiah's followers scatter
    a. Zechariah 13:7 Matthew 21:37

//Maps//

These maps are highly detailed, and the best I could find online. Probably the best, high resolution maps illustrating the Bible now in the public domain. Feel free to print these in any size you like. There is not copyright.

ATLAS

HISTORICAL GEOGRAPHY

HOLY LAND

GEORGE ADAM SMITH, D.D., LL.D., Litt.D.

J. G. BARTHOLOMEW, LL.D., F.R.S.E., F.R.G.S.

LONDON

HODDER AND STOUGHTON

WARWICK SQUARE, E.C.

MCMXV

http://www.godweb.org/SmithBibleAtlas/index.htm

Straight Through the Bible Reading Plan

1-Jan Genesis 1-3
2-Jan Genesis 4-7
3-Jan Genesis 8:1-11:9
4-Jan Genesis 11:10-14:13
5-Jan Genesis 14:14-18:8
6-Jan Genesis 18:9-21:21
7-Jan Genesis 21:22-24:27
8-Jan Genesis 24:28-26:35
9-Jan Genesis 27-29
10-Jan Genesis 30:1-31:42
11-Jan Genesis 31:43-34:31
12-Jan Genesis 35:1-37:24
13-Jan Genesis 37:25-40:8
14-Jan Genesis 40:9-42:28
15-Jan Genesis 42:29-45:15
16-Jan Genesis 45:16-48:7
17-Jan Genesis 48:8-50:26; Exodus 1
18-Jan Exodus 2:1-5:9
19-Jan Exodus 5:10-8:15
20-Jan Exodus 8:16-11:10
21-Jan Exodus 12:1-14:20
22-Jan Exodus 14:21-17:16
23-Jan Exodus 18:1-21:21
24-Jan Exodus 21:22-25:9
25-Jan Exodus 25:10-27:21
26-Jan Exodus 28-29
27-Jan Exodus 30-32
28-Jan Exodus 33:1-35:29
29-Jan Exodus 35:30-37:2
30-Jan Exodus 38:1-40:16
31-Jan Exodus 40:17-38; Leviticus 1-4
1-Feb Leviticus 5-7
2-Feb Leviticus 8:1-11:8
3-Feb Leviticus 11:9-13:39
4-Feb Leviticus 13:40-14:57
5-Feb Leviticus 15:1-18:18
6-Feb Leviticus 18:19-21:24
7-Feb Leviticus 22-23
8-Feb Leviticus 24:1-26:13
9-Feb Leviticus 26:14-27:34; Numbers 1:1-41
10-Feb Numbers 1:42-3:32
11-Feb Numbers 3:33-5:22
12-Feb Numbers 5:23-7:59
13-Feb Numbers 7:60-10:10
14-Feb Numbers 10:11-13:16

15-Feb Numbers 13:17-15:21

16-Feb Numbers 15:22-16:50

17-Feb Numbers 17-20

18-Feb Numbers 21-23

19-Feb Numbers 24:1-26:34

20-Feb Numbers 26:35-28:31

21-Feb Numbers 29:1-31:47

22-Feb Numbers 31:48-33:56

23-Feb Numbers 34-36; Deuteronomy 1:1-15

24-Feb Deuteronomy 1:16-3:29

25-Feb Deuteronomy 4:1-6:15

26-Feb Deuteronomy 6:16-9:21

27-Feb Deuteronomy 9:22-12:32

28-Feb Deuteronomy 13:1-16:8

1-Mar Deuteronomy 16:9-19:21

2-Mar Deuteronomy 20:1-23:14

3-Mar Deuteronomy 23:15-27:10

4-Mar Deuteronomy 27:11-28:68

5-Mar Deuteronomy 29:1-32:14

6-Mar Deuteronomy 32:15-34:12; Joshua 1:1-9

7-Mar Joshua 1:10-4:24

8-Mar Joshua 5:1-8:23

9-Mar Joshua 8:24-11:9

10-Mar Joshua 11:10-14:15

11-Mar Joshua 15-17

12-Mar Joshua 18:1-21:12

13-Mar Joshua 21:13-23:16

14-Mar Joshua 24; Judges 1-2

15-Mar Judges 3-5

16-Mar Judges 6-7

17-Mar Judges 8-9

18-Mar Judges 10-13

19-Mar Judges 14-16

20-Mar Judges 17:1-20:11

21-Mar Judges 20:12-21:25; Ruth 1:1-2:13

22-Mar Ruth 2:14-4:22; 1Samuel 1

23-Mar 1Samuel 2-4

24-Mar 1Samuel 5:1-9:10

25-Mar 1Samuel 9:11-12:18

26-Mar 1Samuel 12:19-14:42

27-Mar 1Samuel 14:43-17:25

28-Mar 1Samuel 17:26-19:24

29-Mar 1Samuel 20-22

30-Mar 1Samuel 23:1-25:31

31-Mar 1Samuel 25:32-30:10

1-Apr 1Samuel 30:11-31:13; 2Samuel 1-2

2-Apr 2Samuel 3:1-6:11

3-Apr 2Samuel 6:12-10:19

4-Apr 2Samuel 11-13

5-Apr 2Samuel 14-16

6-Apr 2Samuel 17-19

7-Apr 2Samuel 20:1-22:34

8-Apr 2Samuel 22:35-24:17

9-Apr 2Samuel 24:18-25; 1Kings 1:1-2:18

10-Apr 1Kings 2:19-4:19

11-Apr 1Kings 4:20-7:39

12-Apr 1Kings 7:40-9:9

13-Apr 1Kings 9:10-11:25

14-Apr 1Kings 11:26-13:34

15-Apr 1Kings 14-17

16-Apr 1Kings 18:1-20:25

17-Apr 1Kings 20:26-22:36

18-Apr 1Kings 22:37-53; 2Kings 1:1-4:28

19-Apr 2Kings 4:29-8:15

20-Apr 2Kings 8:16-10:24

21-Apr 2Kings 10:25-14:10

22-Apr 2Kings 14:11-17:18

23-Apr 2Kings 17:19-19:24

24-Apr 2Kings 19:25-23:9

25-Apr 1Kings 23:10-25; 1Chronicles 1:1-16

26-Apr 1Chronicles 1:17-3:9

27-Apr 1Chronicles 3:10-6:30

28-Apr 1Chronicles 6:31-8:28

29-Apr 1Chronicles 8:29-11:21

30-Apr 1Chronicles 11:22-15:29

1-May 1Chronicles 16:1-19:9

2-May 1Chronicles 19:10-23:11

3-May 1Chronicles 23:12-26:19

4-May 1Chronicles 26:20-29:19

5-May 1Chronicles 29:20-30; 2Chronicles

1:1-4:10

6-May 2Chronicles 4:11-7:22

7-May 2Chronicles 8:1-11:12

8-May 2Chronicles 11:13-15:19

9-May 2Chronicles 16:1-20:13

10-May 2Chronicles 20:14-24:14

11-May 2Chronicles 24:15-28:27

12-May 2Chronicles 29-31

13-May 2Chronicles 32:1-35:19

14-May 2Chronicles 35:20-36:23; Ezra 1-3

15-May Ezra 4-7

16-May Ezra 8-10; Nehemiah 1

17-May Nehemiah 2-5

18-May Nehemiah 6:1-8:8

19-May Nehemiah 8:9-11:21

20-May Nehemiah 11:22-13:22

21-May Nehemiah 13:23-31; Esther 1-4

22-May Esther 5-10

23-May Job 1:1-5:16

24-May Job 5:17-8:22

25-May Job 9:1-12:12

26-May Job 12:13-16:10

27-May Job 16:11-20:11

28-May Job 20:12-24:12

29-May Job 24:13-29:13

30-May Job 29:14-32:10

31-May Job 32:11-35:16

1-Jun Job 36:1-39:12

2-Jun Job 39:13-42:9

3-Jun Job 42:10-17; Psalms 1:1-5:7

4-Jun Psalms 5:8-8:9

5-Jun Psalms 9-10

6-Jun Psalms 11:1-17:5

7-Jun Psalms 17:6-18:36

8-Jun Psalms 18:37-21:13

9-Jun Psalms 22:1-24:6

10-Jun Psalms 24:7-27:6

11-Jun Psalms 27:7-31:5

12-Jun Psalms 31:6-33:5

13-Jun Psalms 33:6-35:21

14-Jun Psalms 35:22-37:26

15-Jun Psalms 37:27-39:13

16-Jun Psalms 40-42

17-Jun Psalms 43:1-45:12

18-Jun Psalms 45:13-48:14

19-Jun Psalms 49:1-51:9

20-Jun Psalms 51:10-54:7

21-Jun Psalms 55:1-57:3

22-Jun Psalms 57:4-60:12

23-Jun Psalms 61-64

24-Jun Psalms 65:1-68:4

25-Jun Psalms 68:5-69:4

26-Jun Psalms 69:5-71:16

27-Jun Psalms 71:17-73:20

28-Jun Psalms 73:21-76:7

29-Jun Psalms 76:8-78:24

30-Jun Psalms 78:25-72

1-Jul Psalms 79-82

2-Jul Psalms 83-86

3-Jul Psalms 87:1-89:37

4-Jul Psalms 89:38-91:13

5-Jul Psalms 91:14-94:16

6-Jul Psalms 94:17-98:3

7-Jul Psalms 98:4-102:7

8-Jul Psalms 102:8-104:4

9-Jul Psalms 104:5-105:24

10-Jul Psalms 105:25-106:33

11-Jul Psalms 106:34-107:38

12-Jul Psalms 107:39-109:31

13-Jul Psalms 110-113

14-Jul Psalms 114:1-118:9

15-Jul Psalms 118:10-119:40

16-Jul Psalms 119:41-96

17-Jul Psalms 119:97-160

18-Jul Psalms 119:161-124:8

19-Jul Psalms 125-131

20-Jul Psalms 132:1-135:14

21-Jul Psalms 135:15-138:3

22-Jul Psalms 138:4-140:13

23-Jul Psalms 141:1-145:7

24-Jul Psalms 145:8-148:6

25-Jul Psalms 148:7-150:6; Proverbs 1:1-2:9

26-Jul Proverbs 2:10-5:14

27-Jul Proverbs 5:15-8:11

28-Jul Proverbs 8:12-11:11

29-Jul Proverbs 11:12-13:25

30-Jul Proverbs 14-16

31-Jul Proverbs 17-20

1-Aug Proverbs 21-23

2-Aug Proverbs 24:1-27:10

3-Aug Proverbs 27:11-30:33

4-Aug Proverbs 31; Ecclesiastes 1:1-3:8

5-Aug Ecclesiastes 3:9-8:17

6-Aug Ecclesiastes 9-12; Song 1-2

7-Aug Song 3-8; Isaiah 1:1-9

8-Aug Isaiah 1:10-5:17

9-Aug Isaiah 5:18-9:12

10-Aug Isaiah 9:13-13:16
11-Aug Isaiah 13:17-19:10
12-Aug Isaiah 19:11-24:6
13-Aug Isaiah 24:7-28:22
14-Aug Isaiah 28:23-32:20
15-Aug Isaiah 33:1-37:29
16-Aug Isaiah 37:30-40:31
17-Aug Isaiah 41-44
18-Aug Isaiah 45-49
19-Aug Isaiah 50-54
20-Aug Isaiah 55:1-60:9
21-Aug Isaiah 60:10-65:25
22-Aug Isaiah 66; Jeremiah 1:1-2:25
23-Aug Jeremiah 2:26-5:19
24-Aug Jeremiah 5:20-8:22
25-Aug Jeremiah 9-12
26-Aug Jeremiah 13:1-16:9
27-Aug Jeremiah 16:10-20:18
28-Aug Jeremiah 21-24
29-Aug Jeremiah 25-27
30-Aug Jeremiah 28:1-31:20
31-Aug Jeremiah 31:21-33:26
1-Sep Jeremiah 34-36
2-Sep Jeremiah 37:1-41:10
3-Sep Jeremiah 41:11-45:5
4-Sep Jeremiah 46-48
5-Sep Jeremiah 49:1-51:10
6-Sep Jeremiah 51:11-52:34
7-Sep Lamentations 1:1-3:51
8-Sep Lamentations 3:52-5:22; Ezekiel 1-2
9-Sep Ezekiel 3-8
10-Sep Ezekiel 9-12
11-Sep Ezekiel 13:1-16:43
12-Sep Ezekiel 16:44-20:17
13-Sep Ezekiel 20:18-22:12
14-Sep Ezekiel 22:13-24:27
15-Sep Ezekiel 25:1-28:10
16-Sep Ezekiel 28:11-31:18
17-Sep Ezekiel 32:1-34:24
18-Sep Ezekiel 34:25-38:9
19-Sep Ezekiel 38:10-40:49
20-Sep Ezekiel 41-43
21-Sep Ezekiel 44-47
22-Sep Ezekiel 48; Daniel 1:1-2:30
23-Sep Daniel 2:31-4:27
24-Sep Daniel 4:28-7:12
25-Sep Daniel 7:13-11:13
26-Sep Daniel 11:14-12:13; Hosea 1-3
27-Sep Hosea 4-9

28-Sep Hosea 10-14; Joel 1:1-2:17

29-Sep Joel 2:18-3:21; Amos 1-4

30-Sep Amos 5-9; Obadiah 1:1-9

1-Oct Obadiah 1:10-21; Jonah; Micah 1-3

2-Oct Micah 4-7; Nahum 1-2

3-Oct Nahum 3; Habakkuk; Zephaniah 1:1-13

4-Oct Zephaniah 1:14-3:20; Haggai;

Zechariah 1:1-11

5-Oct Zechariah 1:12-7:14

6-Oct Zechariah 8-13

7-Oct Zechariah 14; Malachi

8-Oct Matthew 1-4

9-Oct Matthew 5-7

10-Oct Matthew 8:1-10:15

11-Oct Matthew 10:16-12:21

12-Oct Matthew 12:22-14:12

13-Oct Matthew 14:13-17:13

14-Oct Matthew 17:14-20:34

15-Oct Matthew 21-22

16-Oct Matthew 23:1-25:13

17-Oct Matthew 25:14-26:68

18-Oct Matthew 26:69-28:20

19-Oct Mark 1-3

20-Oct Mark 4-5

21-Oct Mark 6-7

22-Oct Mark 8:1-10:12

23-Oct Mark 10:13-12:12

24-Oct Mark 12:13-14:11

25-Oct Mark 14:12-15:47

26-Oct Mark 16; Luke 1

27-Oct Luke 2-3

28-Oct Luke 4:1-6:26

29-Oct Luke 6:27-8:25

30-Oct Luke 8:26-10:16

31-Oct Luke 10:17-12:12

1-Nov Luke 12:13-14:11

2-Nov Luke 14:12-16:31

3-Nov Luke 17:1-19:27

4-Nov Luke 19:28-21:9

5-Nov Luke 21:10-22:46

6-Nov Luke 22:47-24:23

7-Nov Luke 24:24-53; John 1:1-2:11

8-Nov John 2:12-4:38

9-Nov John 4:39-6:51

10-Nov John 6:52-8:20

11-Nov John 8:21-10:18

12-Nov John 10:19-12:11

13-Nov John 12:12-14:11

14-Nov John 14:12-17:13

15-Nov John 17:14-19:42

16-Nov John 20-21; Acts 1:1-2:13

17-Nov Acts 2:14-4:37

18-Nov Acts 5:1-7:29

19-Nov Acts 7:30-9:22

20-Nov Acts 9:23-11:30

21-Nov Acts 12-13

22-Nov Acts 14:1-16:10

23-Nov Acts 16:11-18:28

24-Nov Acts 19-20

25-Nov Acts 21:1-23:25

26-Nov Acts 23:26-27:8

27-Nov Acts 27:9-28:31; Romans 1:1-15

28-Nov Romans 1:16-5:11

29-Nov Romans 5:12-8:25

30-Nov Romans 8:26-11:24

1-Dec Romans 11:25-15:33

2-Dec Romans 16; 1Corinthians 1:1-4:13

3-Dec 1Corinthians 4:14-7:40

4-Dec 1Corinthians 8:1-12:11

5-Dec 1Corinthians 12:12-15:28

6-Dec 1Corinthians 15:29-16:24;

2Corinthians 1-2

7-Dec 2Corinthians 3-7

8-Dec 2Corinthians 8-12

9-Dec 2Corinthians 13; Galatians 1:1-4:11

10-Dec Galatians 4:12-6:18; Ephesians 1:1-14

11-Dec Ephesians 1:15-5:14

12-Dec Ephesians 5:15-6:24; Phillipians 1-2

13-Dec Phillipians 3-4; Colossians 1

14-Dec Colossians 2-4; 1Thessalonians 1:1-

2:12

15-Dec 1Thessalonians 2:13-5:28;

2Thessalonians

16-Dec 1Timothy 1-5

17-Dec 1Timothy 6; 2Timothy

18-Dec Titus; Philemon; Hebrews 1:1-2:10

19-Dec Hebrews 2:11-6:20

20-Dec Hebrews 7-10

21-Dec Hebrews 11-13

22-Dec James 1:1-4:10

23-Dec James 4:11-5:20; 1Peter 1:1-3:12

24-Dec 1Peter 3:13-5:14; 2Peter 1-2

25-Dec 2Peter 3; 1John 1:1-3:12

26-Dec 1John 3:13-5:21; 2John; 3John; Jude

1:1-16

27-Dec Jude 1:17-25; Revelation 1-4

28-Dec Revelation 5:1-9:11

29-Dec Revelation 9:12-14:8

30-Dec Revelation 14:9-18:24

31-Dec Revelation 19-22

Chronological Bible Reading Plan

Jan 1 Gen 1-3
Jan 2 Gen 4-7
Jan 3 Gen 8-11
Jan 4 Job 1-5
Jan 5 Job 6-9
Jan 6 Job 10-13
Jan 7 Job 14-16
Jan 8 Job 17-20
Jan 9 Job 21-23
Jan 10 Job 24-28
Jan 11 Job 29-31
Jan 12 Job 32-34
Jan 13 Job 35-37
Jan 14 Job 38-39
Jan 15 Job 40-42
Jan 16 Gen 12-15
Jan 17 Gen 16-18
Jan 18 Gen 19-21
Jan 19 Gen 22-24
Jan 20 Gen 25-26
Jan 21 Gen 27-29
Jan 22 Gen 30-31
Jan 23 Gen 32-34
Jan 24 Gen 35-37
Jan 25 Gen 38-40
Jan 26 Gen 41-42
Jan 27 Gen 43-45
Jan 28 Gen 46-47
Jan 29 Gen 48-50
Jan 30 Ex 1-3
Jan 31 Ex 4-6
Feb 1 Ex 7-9
Feb 2 Ex 10-12
Feb 3 Ex 13-15
Feb 4 Ex 16-18
Feb 5 Ex 19-21
Feb 6 Ex 22-24
Feb 7 Ex 25-27
Feb 8 Ex 28-29
Feb 9 Ex 30-32
Feb 10 Ex 33-35
Feb 11 Ex 36-38
Feb 12 Ex 39-40
Feb 13 Lev 1-4
Feb 14 Lev 5-7
Feb 15 Lev 8-10
Feb 16 Lev 11-13
Feb 17 Lev 14-15

Feb 18 Lev 16-18
Feb 19 Lev 19-21
Feb 20 Lev 22-23
Feb 21 Lev 24-25
Feb 22 Lev 26-27
Feb 23 Num 1-2
Feb 24 Num 3-4
Feb 25 Num 5-6
Feb 26 Num 7
Feb 27 Num 8-10
Feb 28 Num 11-13
Mar 1 Num 14-15, Ps 90
Mar 2 Num 16-17
Mar 3 Num 18-20
Mar 4 Num 21-22
Mar 5 Num 23-25
Mar 6 Num 26-27
Mar 7 Num 28-30
Mar 8 Num 31-32
Mar 9 Num 33-34
Mar 10 Num 35-36
Mar 11 Deut 1-2
Mar 12 Deut 3-4
Mar 13 Deut 5-7
Mar 14 Deut 8-10
Mar 15 Deut 11-13
Mar 16 Deut 14-16
Mar 17 Deut 17-20
Mar 18 Deut 21-23
Mar 19 Deut 24-27
Mar 20 Deut 28-29
Mar 21 Deut 30-31
Mar 22 Deut 32-34, Ps 91
Mar 23 Josh 1-4
Mar 24 Josh 5-8
Mar 25 Josh 9-11
Mar 26 Josh 12-15
Mar 27 Josh 16-18
Mar 28 Josh 19-21
Mar 29 Josh 22-24
Mar 30 Judg 1-2
Mar 31 Judg 3-5
Apr 1 Judg 6-7
Apr 2 Judg 8-9
Apr 3 Judg 10-12
Apr 4 Judg 13-15
Apr 5 Judg 16-18
Apr 6 Judg 19-21
Apr 7 Ruth 1-4
Apr 8 1 Sam 1-3
Apr 9 1 Sam 4-8
Apr 10 1 Sam 9-12
Apr 11 1 Sam 13-14
Apr 12 1 Sam 15-17

Apr 13 1 Sam 18-20, Ps 11, Ps 59

Apr 14 1 Sam 21-24

Apr 15 Ps 7, Ps 27, Ps 31, Ps 34, Ps 52

Apr 16 Ps 56, Ps 120, Ps 140-142

Apr 17 1 Sam 25-27

Apr 18 Ps 17, Ps 35, Ps 54, Ps 63

Apr 19 1 Sam 28-31, Ps 18

Apr 20 Ps 121, Ps 123-125, Ps 128-130

Apr 21 2 Sam 1-4

Apr 22 Ps 6, Ps 8-10, Ps 14, Ps 16, Ps 19,Ps 21

Apr 23 1 Chr 1-2

Apr 24 Ps 43-45, Ps 49, Ps 84-85, Ps 87

Apr 25 1 Chr 3-5

Apr 26 Ps 73, Ps 77-78

Apr 27 1 Chr 6

Apr 28 Ps 81, Ps 88, Ps 92-93

Apr 29 1 Chr 7-10

Apr 30 Ps 102-104

May 1 2 Sam 5:1-10, 1 Chr 11-12

May 2 Ps 133

May 3 Ps 106-107

May 4 2 Sam 5:11-6:23, 1 Chr 13-16

May 5 Ps 1-2, Ps 15, Ps 22-24, Ps 47, Ps 68

May 6 Ps 89, Ps 96, Ps 100, Ps 101, Ps 105,Ps 132

May 7 2 Sam 7, 1 Chr 17

May 8 Ps 25, Ps 29, Ps 33, Ps 36, Ps 39

May 9 2 Sam 8-9, 1 Chr 18

May 10 Ps 50, Ps 53, Ps 60, Ps 75

May 11 2 Sam 10, 1 Chr 19, Ps 20

May 12 Ps 65-67, Ps 69-70

May 13 2 Sam 11-12, 1 Chr 20

May 14 Ps 32, Ps 51, Ps 86, Ps 122

May 15 2 Sam 13-15

May 16 Ps 3-4, Ps 12-13, Ps 28, Ps 55

May 17 2 Sam 16-18

May 18 Ps 26, Ps 40, Ps 58, Ps 61-62, Ps 64

May 19 2 Sam 19-21

May 20 Ps 5, Ps 38, Ps 41-42

May 21 2 Sam 22-23, Ps 57

May 22 Ps 95, Ps 97-99

May 23 2 Sam 24, 1 Chr 21-22, Ps 30

May 24 Ps 108-110

May 25 1 Chr 23-25

May 26 Ps 131, Ps 138-139, Ps 143-145

May 27 1 Chr 26-29, Ps 127

May 28 Ps 111-118

May 29 1 Kgs 1-2, Ps 37, Ps 71, Ps 94

May 30 Ps 119:1-88

May 31 1 Kgs 3-4, 2 Chr 1, Ps 72

Jun 1 Ps 119:89-176

Jun 2 Sng 1-8

Jun 3 Prov 1-3

Jun 4 Prov 4-6

Jun 5 Prov 7-9

Jun 6 Prov 10-12

Jun 7 Prov 13-15

Jun 8 Prov 16-18

Jun 9 Prov 19-21

Jun 10 Prov 22-24

Jun 11 1 Kgs 5-6, 2 Chr 2-3

Jun 12 1 Kgs 7, 2 Chr 4

Jun 13 1 Kgs 8, 2 Chr 5

Jun 14 2 Chr 6-7, Ps 136

Jun 15 Ps 134, Ps 146-150

Jun 16 1 Kgs 9, 2 Chr 8

Jun 17 Prov 25-26

Jun 18 Prov 27-29

Jun 19 Eccl 1-6

Jun 20 Eccl 7-12

Jun 21 1 Kgs 10-11, 2 Chr 9

Jun 22 Prov 30-31

Jun 23 1 Kgs 12-14

Jun 24 2 Chr 10-12

Jun 25 1 Kgs 15:1-24, 2 Chr 13-16

Jun 26 1 Kgs 15:25-16:34, 2 Chr 17

Jun 27 1 Kgs 17-19

Jun 28 1 Kgs 20-21

Jun 29 1 Kgs 22, 2 Chr 18

Jun 30 2 Chr 19-23

Jul 1 Obad 1, Ps 82-83

Jul 2 2 Kgs 1-4

Jul 3 2 Kgs 5-8

Jul 4 2 Kgs 9-11

Jul 5 2 Kgs 12-13, 2 Chr 24

Jul 6 2 Kgs 14, 2 Chr 25

Jul 7 Jonah 1-4

Jul 8 2 Kgs 15, 2 Chr 26

Jul 9 Isa 1-4

Jul 10 Isa 5-8

Jul 11 Amos 1-5

Jul 12 Amos 6-9

Jul 13 2 Chr 27, Isa 9-12

Jul 14 Mic 1-7

Jul 15 2 Chr 28, 2 Kgs 16-17

Jul 16 Isa 13-17

Jul 17 Isa 18-22

Jul 18 Isa 23-27

Jul 19 2 Kgs 18:1-8, 2 Chr 29-31, Ps 48

Jul 20 Hos 1-7

Jul 21 Hos 8-14

Jul 22 Isa 28-30

Jul 23 Isa 31-34

Jul 24 Isa 35-36

Jul 25 Isa 37-39, Ps 76

Jul 26 Isa 40-43

Jul 27 Isa 44-48

Jul 28 2 Kgs 18:9-19:37, Ps 46, Ps 80, Ps 135

Jul 29 Isa 49-53

Jul 30 Isa 54-58

Jul 31 Isa 59-63

Aug 1 Isa 64-66

Aug 2 2 Kgs 20-21

Aug 3 2 Chr 32-33

Aug 4 Nahum 1-3

Aug 5 2 Kgs 22-23, 2 Chr 34-35

Aug 6 Zeph 1-3

Aug 7 Jer 1-3

Aug 8 Jer 4-6

Aug 9 Jer 7-9

Aug 10 Jer 10-13

Aug 11 Jer 14-17

Aug 12 Jer 18-22

Aug 13 Jer 23-25

Aug 14 Jer 26-29

Aug 15 Jer 30-31

Aug 16 Jer 32-34

Aug 17 Jer 35-37

Aug 18 Jer 38-40, Ps 74, Ps 79

Aug 19 2 Kgs 24-25, 2 Chr 36

Aug 20 Hab 1-3

Aug 21 Jer 41-45

Aug 22 Jer 46-48

Aug 23 Jer 49-50

Aug 24 Jer 51-52

Aug 25 Lam 1:1-3:36

Aug 26 Lam 3:37-5:22

Aug 27 Ezek 1-4

Aug 28 Ezek 5-8

Aug 29 Ezek 9-12

Aug 30 Ezek 13-15

Aug 31 Ezek 16-17

Sep 1 Ezek 18-19

Sep 2 Ezek 20-21

Sep 3 Ezek 22-23

Sep 4 Ezek 24-27

Sep 5 Ezek 28-31

Sep 6 Ezek 32-34

Sep 7 Ezek 35-37

Sep 8 Ezek 38-39

Sep 9 Ezek 40-41

Sep 10 Ezek 42-43

Sep 11 Ezek 44-45

Sep 12 Ezek 46-48

Sep 13 Joel 1-3

Sep 14 Dan 1-3

Sep 15 Dan 4-6

Sep 16 Dan 7-9

Sep 17 Dan 10-12

Sep 18 Ezra 1-3

Sep 19 Ezra 4-6, Ps 137

Sep 20 Hag 1-2

Sep 21 Zech 1-7

Sep 22 Zech 8-14

Sep 23 Est 1-5

Sep 24 Est 6-10

Sep 25 Ezra 7-10

Sep 26 Neh 1-5

Sep 27 Neh 6-7

Sep 28 Neh 8-10

Sep 29 Neh 11-13, Ps 126

Sep 30 Mal 1-4

Oct 1 Luke 1, John 1:1-14

Oct 2 Matt 1, Luke 2:1-38

Oct 3 Matt 2, Luke 2:39-52

Oct 4 Matt 3, Mark 1, Luke 3

Oct 5 Matt 4, Luke 4-5, John 1:15-51

Oct 6 John 2-4

Oct 7 Mark 2

Oct 8 John 5

Oct 9 Matt 12:1-21, Mark 3, Luke 6

Oct 10 Matt 5-7

Oct 11 Matt 8:1-13, Luke 7

Oct 12 Matt 11

Oct 13 Matt 12:22-50, Luke 11

Oct 14 Matt 13, Luke 8

Oct 15 Matt 8:14-34, Mark 4-5

Oct 16 Matt 9-10

Oct 17 Matt 14, Mark 6, Luke 9:1-17

Oct 18 John 6

Oct 19 Matt 15, Mark 7

Oct 20 Matt 16, Mark 8, Luke 9:18-27

Oct 21 Matt 17, Mark 9, Luke 9:28-62

Oct 22 Matt 18

Oct 23 John 7-8

Oct 24 John 9:1-10:21

Oct 25 Luke 10-11, John 10:22-42

Oct 26 Luke 12-13

Oct 27 Luke 14-15

Oct 28 Luke 16-17:10

Oct 29 John 11

Oct 30 Luke 17:11-18:14

Oct 31 Matt 19, Mark 10

Nov 1 Matt 20-21

Nov 2 Luke 18:15-19:48

Nov 3 Mark 11, John 12

Nov 4 Matt 22, Mark 12

Nov 5 Matt 23, Luke 20-21

Nov 6 Mark 13

Nov 7 Matt 24

Nov 8 Matt 25

Nov 9 Matt 26, Mark 14

Nov 10 Luke 22, John 13

Nov 11 John 14-17

Nov 12 Matt 27, Mark 15

Nov 13 Luke 23, John 18-19

Nov 14 Matt 28, Mark 16

Nov 15 Luke 24, John 20-21

Nov 16 Acts 1-3

Nov 17 Acts 4-6

Nov 18 Acts 7-8

Nov 19 Acts 9-10

Nov 20 Acts 11-12

Nov 21 Acts 13-14

Nov 22 Acts 15-16

Nov 23 Acts 17-18:18

Nov 24 Acts 18:19-19:41

Nov 25 Acts 20-23

Nov 26 Acts 24-26

Nov 27 Acts 27-28

Nov 28 Jas 1-5

Nov 29 1 Cor 1-4

Nov 30 1 Cor 5-8

Dec 1 1 Cor 9-11

Dec 2 1 Cor 12-14

Dec 3 1 Cor 15-16

Dec 4 2 Cor 1-4

Dec 5 2 Cor 5-9

Dec 6 2 Cor 10-13

Dec 7, Rom 1-3

Dec 8 Rom 4-7

Dec 9 Rom 8-10

Dec 10 Rom 11-13

Dec 11 Rom 14-16

Dec 12 1 Thes 1-5, 2 Thes 1-3

Dec 13 Gal 1-3

Dec 14 Gal 4-6

Dec 15 Col 1-4, Phm 1

Dec 16 Eph 1-6

Dec 17 Phil 1-4

Dec 18 1 Tim 1-6

Dec 19 Titus 1-3

Dec 20 1 Pet 1-5

Dec 21 Heb 1-6

Dec 22 Heb 7-10

Dec 23 Heb 11-13

Dec 24 2 Tim 1-4

Dec 25 2 Pet 1-3, Jude 1

Dec 26 1 Jn 1-5

Dec 27 2 Jn 1, 3 Jn 1

Dec 28 Rev 1-5

Dec 29 Rev 6-11

Dec 30 Rev 12-18

Dec 31 Rev 19-22

Freebies for you.

- Printable End Resources
- Kid's Hacks
- Shareable Version of HYB
- Workshop Hand Outs/ Helps
- Video Demos

Go to http://eepurl.com/GHH_T

or scan this QR code:

Sign up and we'll put the freebies in your email inbox immediately!

Made in the USA
Middletown, DE
26 March 2018